100 Ideas for
Early Years Practitioners

Supporting EAL Learners

Other titles in the 100 Ideas for Early Years Practitioners series:

100 Ideas for Early Years Practitioners: Outstanding Practice
by Lucy Peet

100 Ideas for Early Years Practitioners: School Readiness
by Clare Ford

100 Ideas for Early Years Practitioners: Outdoor Play
by Julie Mountain

100 Ideas for Early Years Practitioners

Supporting EAL Learners

Marianne Sargent

B L O O M S B U R Y

LONDON • OXFORD • NEW YORK • NEW DELHI • SYDNEY

Bloomsbury Education
An imprint of Bloomsbury Publishing Plc

50 Bedford Square
London
WC1B 3DP
UK

1385 Broadway
New York
NY 10018
USA

www.bloomsbury.com

First published 2016

British Library Cataloguing-in-Publication Data
A catalogue record for this book is available from the British Library.

ISBN:
PB 9781472924056
ePub 9781472924070
ePDF 9781472924063

Library of Congress Cataloging-in-Publication Data
A catalog record for this book is available from the Library of Congress.

10 9 8 7 6 5 4

Typeset by Newgen Knowledge Works (P) Ltd., Chennai, India
Printed and bound in
CPI Group (UK) Ltd, Croydon, CR0 4YY

This book is produced using paper that is made from wood grown in
managed, sustainable forests. It is natural, renewable and recyclable. The
logging and manufacturing processes conform to the environmental
regulations of the country of origin.

To view more of our titles please visit www.bloomsbury.com

Contents

Acknowledgements

As always I could not have written this book without the love and support of my husband Ged and beautiful little boy Harry.

Thanks also to all the different early years practitioners and teachers that I have worked with over the years, and in particular to the following people who inspired a number of the 100 ideas in this book.

Ideas 1, 2, 5, 24, 25, 33, 91 and 93: All of these ideas come from my experience of working with the ultra-organised and efficient Cat Farnon and Kathryn Mahrer at First Tower Primary School in Jersey.

Ideas 23 and 30 come from my son's reception teacher Vicki Cawthorn at Chinley Primary School, Derbyshire. The quote for idea 30 is from my son Harry and is something that he said to me regularly throughout his reception year.

Idea 51: This was the brainchild of my first classroom assistant Annette Caprani, who carried me through my NQT year as a reception teacher.

Ideas 55 and 77: I first came across these ideas when attending training led by the inspirational Ros Bayley back in 2006. I have used the ice provocation in several different guises over the years since, and found it particularly effective for exciting and motivating three-year-old Madeiran children learning EAL.

Introduction

Providing for children who are learning English as an additional language (EAL) is complex and challenging, particularly if you are catering for several children who speak different languages. This book provides guidance for students and early years practitioners who are at the beginning of their careers, as well as more experienced practitioners who find themselves working with EAL learners for the first time. It aims to give advice about how best to provide for children who are new to English as well as example activity ideas that can be taken straight from the page or adapted to suit.

Working with children who are learning EAL is not just about language, it is also about identity and culture. In order to provide for these children you need to create a welcoming and inclusive learning environment where all cultures are respected and valued and all children feel comfortable, secure and proud of their linguistic heritage. Therefore, the beginning of this book aims to give you plenty of ideas about how to help new starters settle and fit into their new early years setting. In addition, there is a section about how you can support and include parents of EAL learners, while throughout the book there are further ideas for using parents' expertise to help within the setting and develop EAL resources.

It is now widely acknowledged that EAL learners should be encouraged to retain and develop their first language for a number of reasons. As well as being part of a child's identity, language is the basis on which their future learning is based. EAL learners come to the early years setting with prior experience of basic concepts and ideas which have been processed in their first language. Practitioners need to use and build on this to introduce the English language and further extend knowledge and understanding. Furthermore, although there may be some degree of delay initially, bilingual children are more likely to make faster progress in the future because their linguistic knowledge will be a cognitive advantage (British Council, 2015). The teaching and activity ideas throughout this book are devised with this in mind. There are reminders throughout to start with what each child knows, look for what they are interested in and use their first language as a gateway to further learning. In the early years EAL learners need much the same as other young children, namely active, hands-on activities that enable them to link language to first-hand experience.

Finally the book concludes with ideas and guidance on how to assess and plan for children learning EAL. There is advice about how you can plan to ensure that EAL learners have equal access to the curriculum as well as pointers for how to identify children who may have learning delay or additional needs. There is also advice about what to look for during observations in order to assess EAL learners' progress.

Children learning EAL have the potential to become high-achieving and successful lifelong learners. I hope this book will give you the confidence to meet the challenge of teaching these children and give them the best start possible.

How to use this book

This book includes quick, easy, practical ideas and guidance for you to dip in and out of to help you provide for young children who are learning EAL.

Each idea includes:

- a catchy title, easy to refer to and share with your colleagues
- a quote from a practitioner, parent or child describing their experience that has led to the idea
- a summary of the idea in bold, making it easy to flick through the book and identify an idea you want to use at a glance
- a step-by-step guide to implementing the idea.

Each idea also includes one or more of the following:

Teaching tip

Practical tips and advice for how and how not to run the activity or put the idea into practice.

Taking it further

Ideas and advice for how to extend the idea or develop it further.

Bonus idea ★

There are 27 bonus ideas in this book that are extra-exciting, extra-original and extra-interesting.

Involving parents

Tips for how to get parents involved in their children's learning, either in the early years setting or at home.

Online resources also accompany this book. When the link to the resource is referenced in the book, follow the link **www.bloomsbury.com/100-ideas-early-years-EAL** to find extra resources, catalogued under the relevant idea number. Here you can also find the full list of website addresses mentioned in the book.

Share how you use these ideas and find out what other practitioners have done using **#100ideas**.

New arrivals

Part 1

Home turf

"Home visits really help new children because you're meeting them on their own turf where they feel most comfortable, safe and secure."

Joining a new setting can be terrifying. Being unable to understand what everyone around you is saying and experiencing new routines and customs can only add to the feeling of isolation. Arriving to be greeted by a friendly and familiar face can be of great comfort, and this is why an initial home visit is so helpful.

Making the effort to visit a new family demonstrates a willingness to build a positive relationship by getting to know them and finding out about their background, culture and customs. The visit is a special occasion for a child, who gets a chance to meet their new key worker or teacher, show them where they live and tell them about the games they like to play. Home visits also help to put parents at ease, hopefully giving them more confidence in their child's new setting and encouraging them to approach practitioners in the future. These visits enable practitioners to build a more rounded picture of a child, giving them insight into certain interests and behaviours that might stem from practices in the home.

- Undertake home visits in pairs, taking with you an assistant from the setting who speaks the child's home language if at all possible. As well as acting as a translator, such an assistant can help to assess the ability of the child to speak and understand their home language.
- Take a basket of toys, books and story bags to share with the child. Ask the child to show you what they like to play with at home. Do they have any favourite or particularly special toys? Do they have a comforter? Does it have a special name?

- Make and take with you a book about the setting. Include photos of the play areas, kitchen, toilets and cloakrooms, as well as children arriving, playing, sitting with their key worker groups and listening to a story. Show this to the child and talk them through what happens on a typical day.
- Ask the parents if the child has any favourite stories or rhymes that they can bring into the setting to share with the other children.
- Compile and take with you a questionnaire to record information about the child and their family. The statutory framework for the EYFS (DfE, 2014) sets out minimum requirements in terms of what information you must collect about each child in your care. In addition to this it is essential to find out about medical requirements, allergies, special needs and disabilities. In the case of a child who speaks EAL it is also helpful find out the following: what the child is normally called at home (check spelling and correct pronunciation); the language(s) the parents usually use to communicate with the child; the language the child prefers to speak; how long the family has been in the county; whether the child has friends or relatives that already attend the setting; whether the child has previously attended a pre-school, nursery or school in their home country; religion, cultural beliefs and celebrations observed; dietary requirements, favourite foods and whether the child is used to using cutlery or fingers; cultural expectations in terms of physical contact, skin care, hair care, toileting, sleeping arrangements/routines and clothing; cultural expectations in terms of how independent the parents expect their child to be; and whether the parents can understand, speak and read English.
- Remember to ask parents about their own feelings, anxieties and questions about their child starting at your setting.

Online resource: home visit questionnaire

3

A good policy

"It helped to just sit down together and think about what we needed to do."

Formulate a policy for working with children who are learning EAL, and ensure all members of staff are fully acquainted with it.

Involving parents

Ensure that parents are given a copy of the policy when their child starts at the setting. Provide translated versions for those parents who cannot read English.

If you are new to EAL you should refer to your setting's policy for information about what is required of you and how you should be working with the children and their families. You will be able to get this from whoever is responsible for coordinating English language learning. However, if your setting does not yet have any children who are learning EAL you may not have such a policy and so will need to compose some guidance that will ensure all members of staff take a consistent approach. An EAL policy should include the following:

- **Introduction:** The purpose and rationale of the policy: what EAL means and why you have decided to take the approach chosen.
- **Aims:** What the policy sets out to do to meet the needs of those children who are learning EAL; to value cultural diversity; to support the continued use of children's home languages; to help children understand, speak, read and write English; to support parents and families; and to assess and monitor progress.
- **Strategies:** How you plan to achieve these aims. How you will: organise, resource and present the learning environment; communicate with parents; create a culturally diverse setting; support the continued use of children's home languages; plan activities that will help with English language learning; and assess the progress of children who are learning EAL.
- **Monitoring and review:** Who has responsibility for ensuring the policy is adhered to and how often it will be reviewed.

Taking it further

The policy should be regularly reviewed and updated so that it reflects the changing needs of the children and their families.

Online resource: example policy

Warm welcome

"He was so happy to see that we had some of his favourite toys to play with."

Make the initial settling-in period easier for a new child by taking steps to ensure that they and their family feel welcome.

Use these ideas to help create a welcoming and inclusive learning environment that will help a new child cope with the initial transition.

- Ensure that any welcome signs at the entrance represent all languages of the children and families in the setting.
- Ensure staff and children can pronounce the new child's name correctly ahead of their arrival. Do not suggest nicknames or shortened versions.
- Learn and teach the children greetings in the new child's home language. Make an effort to use the greeting when the new family arrives.
- Allow the new child to bring in a comforter from home that they can carry around with them during the settling-in period.
- Ask parents about the child's favourite toys and games at home and ensure that similar resources and activities are set up on the day of their arrival.
- Source some dual-language picture books featuring the child's home language from your local library.
- Ensure that the child's key worker knows some key words in the child's home language to help them communicate.
- Provide a familiar food for their snack.
- Ensure that the child is given quality time with their new key worker. Support their key worker by giving them time to assist the child with daily tasks such as self-registration, toileting, accessing resources and helping themselves to their snack.

Involving parents

Invite parents to stay for as long as they feel necessary during the first few visits. Talk to them and help them feel free to voice any worries or concerns.

Taking it further

Make a photo diary of the child's first week at the setting. Include photos of new friends and special people, including their key worker. Write a simple caption under each picture. Send the diary home for the child to share with their parents.

New starters' storybook

"Her dad said they read the book every night for the whole week before she started."

Children respond well to stories, and especially stories that feature other children of the same age. Create a storybook about the play and adventures that children experience in your setting, and use it to give new starters a taste of what to expect before they join.

Many children from other countries will have previous experience of being in a pre-school or early years setting. However, this experience is likely to be very different from that in Britain. A prospectus is a useful way of informing and preparing parents ahead of their child joining a new setting; however, it also helps to produce a child-friendly version in the form of a storybook.

- Take photos of the children and staff in your setting as they participate in daily activities.
- Use the photos to create a story about attending your setting. You can approach this either by focusing on a couple of children and telling the story through their eyes, or creating a general overview with photos of everyone.
- Arrange the photos so they demonstrate the running of a typical day. For example, include children arriving, choosing activities, participating in group time, having lunch, listening to stories, taking part in music and movement, playing outside and going home.
- Write a sentence or two under each picture to describe what is happening, naming members of staff and explaining routines. Have the book translated into the languages of the children due to attend.
- Print and bind a copy for every new starter and give it to them before they begin at your setting.

Visual timetable

"Mummy come soon?"

Make a new child feel safe and secure by giving them a visual timetable to help them develop a sense of time and an understanding of what happens during a typical day at the setting.

A regular routine and sense of time is important for helping young children to feel safe and secure. This is especially true for those children who are new to a country and language, because a strange culture and lack of understanding will only increase their sense of bewilderment. When joining a new early years setting something as simple as a visual timetable can really help, because it will enable these children to keep track of where they are in the day.

- Set up a display board at child height.
- Over the course of a week take photos of the children in your setting engaged in various activities, for example answering the register, playing in different areas of learning, snack time, story time, circle time, music and movement, outdoor play and getting ready to go home. Take additional photos of the target child participating in individual activities.
- Print off and laminate some days of the week and number cards in both English and the child's home language.
- Use hook-and-loop fastener to stick the day of the week and number cards in a row across the top of the board.
- Again, use hook-and-loop fastener to stick the photos underneath the number cards in sequence to show what happens on that particular day.
- Bring the child to the board at the beginning of the day and run through what they will be doing. Then revisit the board frequently to look at what has already happened and what will be happening next.

Teaching tip

Throughout the week use repetitive phrases for specific times of the day, for example story time, tidy-up time, lunchtime, circle time, time to get busy and group time. EAL learners will become familiar with these and will begin to recognise the verbal signals.

Taking it further

Attach a plastic wallet to the display. Invite the child to remove the activities from the board and post them in the wallet once they are completed.

Survival language

"Toilet, please."

Initially it is helpful to give a child who is new to English a bank of 'survival' language that they can use to get by and communicate important needs.

When a child first arrives, one of the main priorities should be to help them learn a bank of key words and phrases that they can use to communicate their needs and feelings to those around them. This is often referred to as 'survival' language and includes the following:

- Social language that will enable a child to communicate with other children, including 'hello', 'goodbye', 'yes', 'no', 'please', 'thank you', 'my name is . . .', 'would you like to play?' and 'friend'.
- Words and phrases that will enable a child to communicate important needs, including 'stop', 'I am hurt/ill/sick/sad/happy/hungry/thirsty', 'I need the toilet', 'I don't understand', 'I like/don't like . . .' and 'where is . . .?'
- Vocabulary associated with the early years setting and daily routines such as, 'story', 'snack', 'wash hands', 'play', 'indoors', 'outside', 'coat', 'sit on the carpet', 'listen', 'group time', 'circle time', 'get busy', 'share', 'kind', 'gentle', 'tidy-up time' and 'home time'.

It helps to provide the child with visual cue cards that they can show practitioners and other children when they are trying to tell them something. These should feature the written word or phrase, both in English and the child's first language, and a picture. Examples are commercially available on websites such as www.twinkl.co.uk.

Buddy up

"We are lucky here really because we have a few children who speak the same language."

Find friends for new children to help them settle in and learn the ropes.

Pair up a new EAL learner with another child who speaks the same language. If this is not possible, ask a confident English-speaking child with good interpersonal skills if they can show the new child around and help them with everyday routines and tasks.

Teaching tip

Ensure that you choose a buddy who is confident yet not too overpowering. Choose someone who is relatively gentle in nature and will give the new child a chance to absorb everything around them and get a word in edgeways!

- Buddying up children who speak the same language will encourage them to continue to use their mother tongue, which is extremely important. However, do not assume that speakers of the same language will also speak in the same dialect. Those EAL learners who have been in the setting for a while will already be speaking some English and so will be able to help new learners communicate with other children in the group.
- An English-speaking buddy will need some key words and phrases. However, avoid putting too much pressure on them and instead teach everyone some key words and phrases in the new child's home language as a matter of course. Introduce vocabulary as you follow regular routines throughout the day.
- Give an English-speaking buddy a hand-held fan of key survival vocabulary (see Idea 6) that they can use to communicate with their new friend.
- When assigning tasks to individuals, ensure that you either pair EAL learners up or put them into small groups with established peers who can show them how things are done.

Feeling different

"Using stories is a great way of exploring issues and feelings with young children."

There are some good-quality picture books that deal with difference and isolation.

Try the following books to help new children settle in as well as to help the other children in the setting understand how they might be feeling.

- *Ten Little Fingers and Ten Little Toes* by Mem Fox and Helen Oxenbury (Walker): Poem about difference with repetitive, rhyming text.
- *Say Hello* by Jack and Michael Foreman (Walker): Story about being left out.
- *Beegu* by Alexis Deacon (Red Fox): Story about feeling different and lonely.
- *Oliver* by Birgitta Sif (Walker): Story about having no friends and feeling lonely.
- *It's Okay to be Different* by Todd Parr (Little, Brown Young Readers): Bright picture book about being different.
- *The Animal Boogie* by Debbie Harter (Barefoot Singalong): Rhythmical, repetitive text with singalong CD, which represents children of different ethnic backgrounds in the pictures.
- *Smiley Shark* by Ruth Galloway (Little Tiger Press): Story about being left out.
- *Everyone Matters: A First Look at Respect for Others* by Pat Thomas and Lesley Harker (Barron's Educational Series): Issues book that deals with treating everyone fairly and sensitively.
- *Blue Chameleon* by Emily Gravett (Macmillan): Story with very few words about being proud of who you are.
- *Mr Big* by Ed Vere (Puffin): Story with bold pictures about not judging a book by its cover.
- *Elmer* by David McKee (Andersen Press): Story about an elephant that looks different to all the others in the herd.

The silent period

"She's barely said two words since she started here six weeks ago."

It is not unusual for a non-English-speaking child to appear silent during the initial settling-in period after arriving in a new setting. However, it is important to keep an eye out for those children who are in danger of withdrawing completely and becoming isolated.

When non-English-speaking children first arrive in a setting they will need time to adjust to their new surroundings. Siraj-Blatchford and Clarke (2000) explain that some such children will remain quiet for the first few days, weeks or even months, communicating through non-verbal signals, facial expressions and body language, and using single-word utterances only when essential. They point out that this is normal and nothing to worry about. All the time these children will be watching and listening and gradually taking in the English language that is being used around them.

However, there are a number of strategies that can be used to ensure that such children do not withdraw completely and risk becoming isolated.

- Place these children in a group with others who speak the same language.
- Assign them to a bilingual key worker who can speak their language.
- Pair them up with other confident and sociable children who will include them in their play.
- Put them in a group and give them a task to do together.
- Find out what interests them and provide toys and resources that they will enjoy using and playing with.

Teaching tip

Just because a child is not speaking it does not mean that they do not understand. Allow quiet children to begin speaking in their own time, whether this is in their home language or English. Do not force the issue – they will talk when they are ready.

11

Parachute games

"Five, four, three, two, one . . . mushroom!"

Parachute games require children to work together as a team, which helps new children to feel valued and included. In addition, children need to listen out for verbal instructions, offering opportunities for English language development.

The mushroom game is a good starting point for parachute play. It is very simple and helps children to practise listening and cooperation. There are also variations that add to the challenge.

- Get the children to spread out evenly around the edge of a large parachute and hold it taut.
- Tell everyone to lower their hands to knee level. When you count down and shout out the magic word they should raise their hands into the air, pulling the parachute upwards. It will fill with air and rise up like a giant mushroom.
- Explain that they can make it rise up higher by taking two steps towards the middle as it rises.
- Practise this a few times until the children can work together in sync to create the mushroom effect.
- The magic word can be anything you like – it could simply be 'mushroom'. Once you have chosen a magic word find out the translation in the different languages your EAL learners speak. Each time you have a go, say the countdown and the magic word in a different language.

My new home

"This is a lovely topic because we go out for walks and to the play park, so not only do the children learn about where they live but they enjoy getting to know their new friends as they explore and play."

Help new arrivals to become familiar with their new home by doing a topic about the local area.

Take the children out and about to explore the place they have moved to.

- Before you leave compile a list of key words that you will need in the children's first languages. Think about what you will come across and the words you are likely to use when naming and talking about shops, buildings and places of interest.
- Go for a walk around the local area. Take a look inside shops and talk about what they sell, and look at local amenities such as launderettes and restaurants and explain what they are for and what they provide. Take a digital camera so you can take photos of landmarks.
- Create a display about the local area. Download an aerial map using a website such as Google Maps (www.google.co.uk/maps) and stick on the photos you took during the walk. Label the photos both in English and other relevant languages.
- Look at the map and trace the route of your walk. Reflect on what you came across and use this as an opportunity to repeat and revise the language and vocabulary introduced on the walk.

Involving parents

Pack a picnic and invite parents to accompany their children on a whole-setting trip to the local play park. Use the trip to teach the children vocabulary associated with food, play equipment and physical movement.

Taking it further

Click on the 'Earth' icon in Google Maps to switch to an aerial photo of the area, and project the image for all the children to see. Use this photo for further language development by asking the children to spot cars, trees, people and train tracks, among other things.

My new home: interactive map

"We use presentation software all the time to make maps, books and presentations with the children. There's something about using computers that makes those less confident children get more involved and want to say more."

Create a multilingual interactive map as a way of consolidating language learned during a walk around the local area. Involve the children in creating the map to give them a chance to revisit the places that they saw and revise the associated vocabulary.

Teaching tip

Enlist the help of a bilingual support assistant to add comments in other languages to the slides. If this is not possible, use the audio recording function to record non-English speakers' verbal comments.

You can use any type of presentation software to create an interactive map. The following instructions can be used for both Microsoft PowerPoint and Keynote for Mac.

Step 1
Help the children take digital photos of landmarks and places of interest while out on a walk around your local area.

Step 2
Use presentation software to set up a template for an interactive map.

Teaching tip

It is possible to type in different language scripts on both Windows and Mac operating systems, and you can find out how to set this up by going to https://support.microsoft.com/en-us or www.apple.com/support. You can also find some useful instructional videos on YouTube.

- Create a title slide with the name of your town or village and a map.
- Download an aerial map of the area on Google Maps and take a screen shot.
- Paste this image on to the slide and crop it so that it only shows the map.
- Create enough additional slides to correspond with the locations you want to identify on the map.
- Add titles to the slides (with translations in relevant languages) and insert the photos you took earlier.
- Insert labels (again with translations) on the map indicating where each place of interest is.

Step 3
Set up hyperlinks between the title slide and the location slides.

- Create hyperlinks between each of the labels on the map and the slides so that when you click on a location label it takes you to the corresponding slide.
- Create a return button on each slide so that when you click on the button it takes you back to the map.

Step 4
Get the children to help add some information.

- Gather the children in small groups, ensuring a mix of English speakers and non-English speakers.
- Spend some time looking at the map on the title slide. Reflect on the walk and trace your finger along the route you took. Pause to point out the places and things you saw along the way and name them in English and other relevant languages.
- Choose and click on a location and ask the group to help you fill in a bit of information about it.
- Prompt the children to name the place and describe its purpose. If it is a place created for children, such as a playground or park, ask them to tell you what they think about it. Is there anything they would improve? Allow children learning EAL to just listen if they want to, and give plenty of praise if they attempt to say anything in English or otherwise.
- Type the children's comments on to the slide, including comments made in other languages.

Taking it further

Put extra photos on each slide showing the inside of each location to prompt more comment from the children.

Bonus idea ★

Use Google Street View to go on a 'drive' around the area. Leave from the setting and drive to each place on the map. Use this to demonstrate the use of directional language as you talk about which way you are heading and turning.

Online resource: template of an interactive map

Valued and included

"He takes a lot of pride in his job and you can see the sense of importance that he feels."

Giving children responsibility is a good way of raising their self-esteem by giving them a purpose and making them feel like part of the community. Children who are trusted to undertake important tasks will gain confidence and this is particularly important for EAL learners, who will benefit from such a boost.

Teaching tip

Think carefully about who will be able to do each task successfully. The whole point is to raise self-esteem and make the children feel useful. Give silent children jobs that do not require them to speak, and more confident children jobs that involve talking. Another idea is to allocate trickier tasks to pairs or groups so that the children can help each other.

Draw up a task chart allocating responsibilities to the children in your setting.

- Set up a large board with a pictorial list of jobs. Think of tasks that EAL learners can complete without having to use the English language, such as sweeping up under the sand tray, washing fruit, cleaning up paints or tidying the book corner.
- Label each job in English and other relevant languages.
- Stick a strip of hook-and-loop fastener alongside each job.
- Print off and laminate named photos of the children or labelled group cards and stick hook-and-loop fastener to the back.
- Place a child or group picture next to each task to show who is responsible for what.
- Change the board around regularly so that the children get to take on different responsibilities.
- As EAL learners become more confident, English speakers give them jobs that require them to speak to others.

Identity and culture

Part 2

Proud to be bilingual

"Her parents are adamant that they want her to speak both Portuguese and English, but I don't want to make it harder for her than it already is."

It is essential that you work with children and their families to ensure that their first language is maintained and developed.

Teaching tip

If possible avoid mixing languages when speaking to an EAL learner. Instead, decide which staff member will communicate in which language. It may be that you decide to speak only in English to the child, while a support assistant only uses the child's first language.

Involving parents

Parents are a very useful resource, so ask them for help. Invite them to come in to read stories, sing and do group work with children in their first languages.

The statutory framework for the EYFS sets out the expectation that practitioners 'must take reasonable steps to provide opportunities for children to develop and use their home language in play and learning, supporting their language development at home' (DfE, 2014).

A child's home language is part of their identity, and retaining it is essential for their future educational development. Therefore, it is important that you support parents in their efforts to maintain their children's ability to speak and understand their first language. In doing so you will need to take the following into consideration:

- Children should be allowed and encouraged to speak in their first language both within the early years setting and at home. Children who are told only to use English will find this message confusing and it may affect their self-esteem, which will in turn impact on their learning. Bilingualism should be celebrated and children should be made to feel proud that they are able to speak and understand more than one language.
- Patterns of language learning will differ greatly between children. Some children may only speak English when at school and nursery. Others will speak English at home with just one parent, while the other parent uses another language. There are also children whose parents will constantly switch

between English and another language, while encouraging their children to do the same. Some children will speak just one other language, while others will be learning two or three, including a different language in religious contexts.

- It is important to know what languages the children in your care are learning, as well as in which circumstances and with whom they use each different language. This will enable you to understand which is the dominant language in a child's life and help you to decide which of the child's home languages to use when supporting their learning in the setting. Ask parents what language(s) they speak at home. Do they use different languages with different family members? Do they use different languages depending on where they are? Which language is dominant in their life? Which language should you use alongside English within the setting?

Taking it further

Consider employing bilingual support staff who can help children to retain, develop and extend their first languages. This is especially important during the first few months as the children adjust to their new surroundings. The support staff can also make bilingual resources, help you to communicate with parents, develop EAL policies, assess the children's language development in their first language and train other staff about language and culture.

My name is . . .

"It is surprising, but sometimes a new child might have been in the setting for weeks and still not know everyone's names."

Children from other countries may have names that are unfamiliar to their English-speaking peers. What's more, new arrivals will be faced with the task of learning a large number of English names.

Teaching tip

Play these games every day for the first few weeks of term or each time a new child arrives in the setting. Change the groups around each day so the children have the chance to become familiar with everyone's names. Start each game with English-speaking children so that EAL learners can watch and listen to the others demonstrating how it is done before it is their turn.

Taking it further

Sing the songs in the different languages of the children in the setting.

Help all the children remember and correctly pronounce each other's names by playing this simple circle game.

- Divide the children into groups of eight or 10, and sit them in a circle.
- Clap and sing together: 'Hello Sally, hello Sally, stand up, clap your hands and give us all a wave.'
- Sally should then stand up, clap hands and wave to everyone, then sit down.
- Move on to the next child and sing: 'Hello Tarik, hello Tarik, stand up, clap your hands and give us all a wave.'
- Repeat until everyone has had a go.

Try these two alternative rhymes that encourage individual verbal responses from the children.

- Adult sings: 'Hello Petra, hello Petra, where are you?' Child responds, 'Here I am, here I am, how do you do?'
- Everyone sings: 'Good morning, good morning, it's a lovely day today. Good morning, good morning to you . . .' Adult points to a child and sings their name, '. . . Alex.' Everyone sings the song again and this time Alex points to another child and sings their name. And so on.

Stories from home

"He looks so proud when we choose a story from his country."

Be fully inclusive by sourcing stories, traditional tales and songs that represent the various countries and cultures of the children in your setting.

Choose stories and books that contain images representing the cultures within your setting so that children can identify with the characters and plots. Choose traditional tales and songs from different cultures to ensure that children from other countries are afforded the opportunity to hear stories that will be familiar to them as well. There is an abundance of multicultural resources available both in print and online. Try the following sources.

- Storynory has a wide selection of free audio traditional tales from around the world (www.storynory.com/category/myths/various-fairy-tales/).
- Letterbox Library sells books that celebrate multiculturalism, equality and diversity (www.letterboxlibrary.com).
- Little Linguist is a supplier of multicultural resources including posters, books and CDs (www.little-linguist.co.uk/multicultural-resources-for-children.html).
- World Stories presents animated stories from around the world narrated both in English and the language of origin (www.worldstories.org.uk/stories/stories).
- *Tam Tam Tambalay!* book and CD by Helen MacGregor includes chants, echo songs, action songs and playground games from around the world with phonetic transliterations, English meanings and sample performances (www.amazon.co.uk/Tam-Tambalay-Helen-MacGregor/dp/0713679204).

Teaching tip

Group children who speak the same language and give them regular story and rhyme times in their home language.

Involving parents

Invite parents who can speak English to come in and tell the whole group some traditional tales from their country of origin.

Bonus idea ★

Ask parents to send in recordings of traditional songs and rhymes in their home language. Play the songs to the children in the setting and invite the children whose language the songs represent to teach everyone. Make the songs freely accessible for the children to listen to on the listening centre.

My story

"He loves looking at pictures of himself."

Work with parents to make a photo book of their child's life story. Share it with their child in the setting to help them settle in, while at the same time aiding their English language development.

Ask parents to send in some photos of their friends and relatives, including those who still live in their home country. Also suggest that they include pictures of their previous home as well as their new one. Get them to write names and places on the back with descriptions of who people are and how they are related. Remember to ensure they that they do not mind the photos being chopped up and stuck with glue.

- Make a booklet out of thin A4 card folded in half and stapled in the middle. Stick a photo on each page.
- Use the information provided by parents to write a simple caption under each photo in English. If possible, get translations of the captions in the child's home language and include these as well.
- Share the book with the child. Give them a chance to tell you what is in the picture in whichever language they prefer. Then read the caption in both languages.
- Point out people and objects and ask the child to name them, then offer English translations.
- Treat the child like an expert and ask them to tell you about specific cultural objects and images in the photos.

Where I come from

"Our children come from many different places and we currently have speakers of 13 different languages."

Celebrate the diversity of cultures within your setting by creating a rolling display that features the place of origin of each of the children in your care.

Set up a 'Where I come from' display and change it regularly to feature each of the children in the group. Change the display termly, weekly or monthly, depending on how many children you have in the setting and the number of different places they come from. Label the display both in English and the language of the featured child.

- Create the display around a world map with colourful pins and a laminated arrow that can be moved each time the display changes.
- Put together a short biography about the child. Include their name, the city, town or village they come from and the language they speak.
- Display pictures of the country that the child comes from, including the flag and famous landmarks. Find out what they like most about where they come from, and display this as a caption.
- Display pictures of produce that comes from their country and foods that they eat. Find out about the child's favourite foods from this place.
- Ask parents if they can send in photos of their home country and relatives who still live there, as well as some interesting objects to show everyone.

Teaching tip

Remember that some children might come from different parts of the same country and speak different languages, as well as have different customs, foods and landscapes. Ensure you also include displays about children who come from different parts of Britain as well as those who come from the local area. This will ensure British children are included and help those who are new to the country learn about the place that they have moved to.

Taking it further

Invite parents to come in and tell the children about the country that they come from.

Representing everyone

"There is a wide variety of multicultural resources available, and we try to make sure that all races and cultures are represented through the resources we provide."

Source toys and resources that reflect the different cultures of the children in your setting.

Make all the children in your setting aware and accepting of difference by providing resources that represent a variety of races and cultures. If children are exposed to images and toys that include people with different skin colours, facial features and clothing they are likely to be less perturbed by the arrival of a child who appears different to them. What's more, the new arrivals will feel more comfortable in a culturally diverse learning environment.

- Buy character puppets that have different skin colours and represent different races.
- Include characters of different races in small world scenes.
- Put clothing from a range of cultures in the dressing up box.
- Fill role-play kitchens with cooking utensils and toy foods that will enable children to re-enact preparing the types of food they eat at home. Provide food packaging that features labels in different languages.
- Place traditional furnishings and ornaments from different cultures and magazines in different languages in the home corner.
- Decorate the home corner so that it represents different cultural celebrations throughout the year.
- Provide translated versions of written role-play resources such as tickets, menus, timetables and maps.
- Source puzzles and games that reflect a range of cultures.

Snack time

"We put all sorts out for snack time. Of course some children don't like to try new foods but that's why it's such a good idea. They see the others eating it and it makes them want to taste it too."

Offer foods from different cultures at snack time to introduce children to a variety of ingredients and flavours.

There are bound to be differences between the eating habits and diets of all the children in your setting. It is very likely there will be even greater differences when you have children from a variety of cultures. It is important to cater for all the children's tastes when deciding what to prepare for snack time. Therefore, find out what types of food the children eat at home and provide these. Not only is this inclusive practice, it is educational for all the children in the group, getting them to experience new tastes while learning about foods from around the world at the same time.

- One option is to focus on foods from one particular culture each day.
- Otherwise, provide a mixture of foods from different cultures every day for the children to pick and choose from.
- Allow those children who do not use cutlery at home to choose whether they use it or not.
- Invite the children to tell each other about the different foods they eat at home and to show everyone how they usually eat them.

Teaching tip

Station an adult at the snack table each morning to facilitate discussion about the different foods. Explain where each food comes from, what the ingredients are and which children in the setting like to eat them at home. Encourage the children to talk about their likes and dislikes.

Remember to ensure that your allergy records are up to date before giving children new or unusual foods.

Bonus idea ★

Invite parents to come into the setting to prepare some traditional dishes with the children. Offer these foods at snack time or have a tasting session and ask the children to discuss their preferences.

Let's celebrate

"We give Eid as much attention as Christmas and Easter because it is celebrated by so many families in our setting."

Invite parents to come in and help plan and prepare celebrations for the different religious festivals celebrated by the children in your setting.

For each festival:

- Invite parents in to talk about the festival. Ask them to share photos and bring in symbolic objects to show to the group.
- Find out if there is a story linked to the festival, and source a child-friendly version to read out.
- Ask parents if there is any particular music that is played at this time. Perhaps they know some songs or rhymes linked to the festival that they can either come in and teach the children or record and send in.
- Ask parents if there are any traditional games that are played during festival celebrations. Perhaps they could come in and teach the children how to play?
- Find out if people send cards during this particular festival, and help the children make some to send to families who are celebrating at the time.
- Find out about decorations that are traditionally used, and help the children make some to decorate the setting.
- Prepare foods that are shared during these particular celebrations. Ask parents if they can send some food in or come in to help prepare some.
- Organise a party and invite all the children's parents to come in and celebrate the festival together.

Taking it further

Create a celebrations display that shows all the different festivals that are celebrated by the children in your setting.

Places of worship

"We are really lucky around here because we have a church, synagogue and temple within our local area."

In order to ensure that children grow up as part of a tolerant society it is important that they learn to respect the views and beliefs of others.

Help the children develop an understanding of different religious beliefs and practices by visiting the places of worship that the families in your setting attend. For each place of worship:

- Before the visit check whether there are any requirements or restrictions with regard to visiting. Do shoes have to be removed? Are there any rules with regard to clothing? Are there areas in the building where only males or females are allowed to enter?
- When you arrive stand outside and take time to look at the architectural design of the building. Point out specific features that have symbolic meaning.
- Find out how often people come to worship in this building, and whether certain days are holy days to people of this particular religion.
- Show the children the book of worship studied by people who practice this particular religion. Look at the script inside. What language is it?
- Find out if people pray inside this building. Where do they pray? What do they do when they pray?
- Look for symbolic objects, artefacts and pictures. What do they mean?
- Provide the children with digital cameras so they can take photos (remember to get permission first). Take note of any comments and observations the children make. These photos and notes can be used to create a display on your return to the setting.

Teaching tip

Do not make assumptions about a family's religion based on where they come from. Instead approach parents by asking what religion, if any, they follow.

Involving parents

Ask parents if they will accompany you on visits to their places of worship and act as guides.

Same difference

"The children were so excited about the wedding and got really involved in planning for the big day."

A topic on weddings is a good way of demonstrating that although people from different cultures do many things differently they also share much in common.

Taking it further

Plan a traditional role-play wedding ceremony at a place of worship or registered premises with the help of a local religious leader or marriage registrar. Invite two parents to re-enact exchanging their vows, while the children take on the roles of the wedding entourage. Ask parents for their advice and guidance with regard to traditional songs, rituals and clothing. Invite parents to the 'wedding' and hold a reception at the setting after.

Find out about how weddings are celebrated in different cultures.

- Invite the children to show and tell about wedding photos from their parents' or other relatives' weddings. Create a display and look at similarities and differences.
- Ask those children who have been to a wedding to recount their experiences. Have any of them ever played a special role?
- Look at traditional foods that are prepared for weddings in different cultures. Ask parents if they can prepare a dish and send it in with an explanation of why it is significant.
- Ask parents to bring in their wedding outfits to show to the children. Source or make small versions for the children to dress up with in the role-play area.
- Set up the role-play area as a place of worship, registry office or premises where wedding ceremonies take place. Change the scene every few days to reflect the different religions and cultures of the children in your setting.
- Examine wedding artefacts from different cultures and faiths, and find out about what they signify.
- Ask parents for examples of the type of music that would traditionally be played at a wedding in their faith or culture.

Bonus idea ★

Visit local places of worship to find out about the different religious faiths of people living in the area.

Working with parents

Part 3

Prospectus

"There are things that are more important to some parents than others so we try to ensure we cover as much as possible in our prospectus."

Ensure that the prospectus for your setting includes information that is useful and relevant to the families of all your children.

When writing a prospectus, as well as including general information about the running of the setting, be sure to include the following:

- **Mission statement:** This should convey that you are a fully inclusive setting.
- **Aims of the setting:** Fostering positive relationships between practitioners, children and families by celebrating diversity.
- **Staff:** Include photos, names and titles of all members of staff, including any additional languages they are able to speak.
- **Admissions policy:** Explain that children who speak EAL will not be discriminated against and will be subject to the same admissions procedures as any other child.
- **Clothing and equipment:** Invite parents to speak to you about any concerns they may have about clothing and religious beliefs.
- **Food and snacks:** Invite parents to speak to you about any concerns they may have about the food that is offered to their children, and personal eating practices at home.
- **Self-care:** Invite parents to speak to you about any concerns they may have about toileting and self-care practices in the setting.
- **Religious beliefs:** Explain that you teach about a range of religions and support individual families' rights to practise their chosen faith.
- **Preparation for starting:** Advice about the types of skills children will need to help them settle in more quickly, such as being able to put on their own shoes and use the toilet independently.

Well informed

"If we are going to put up a parents' display it makes sense that everyone is able to read it."

Ensure that information for parents is accessible and relevant to all.

Create entrance and parents' displays that are fully inclusive by translating signs and notices. In addition, provide translated letters, curriculum guides and prospectuses to ensure that important information is accessible to all parents in your setting.

- Ensure that entrance displays and parent noticeboards feature signs and labels that represent all languages of the children and family in the setting. Multilingual 'welcome' signs are widely available to buy. Also, ask support staff and parents if they can help translate display headers such as 'Snack for today', 'What we are learning', 'Our current topic', and 'Reminders'.
- Put up a 'Who's who' display with photos, names and job titles of every member of staff in the setting so that parents know who to approach when they have a query or problem.
- Where possible, include pictures and symbols on signs, labels and information sheets to make meanings clearer.
- Contact your local authority about obtaining translated information leaflets covering common issues such as head lice.
- Some local authorities also provide translations of common standard letters used by schools and childcare providers. Otherwise Dingle Granby Toxteth Education Action Zone in partnership with the City of Liverpool have produced a wide selection of letters translated into 32 languages. These letters are available free to download (www.primaryresources.co.uk/letters/index. htm) and have been designed so that individual providers can fill in specific details.

Parents as partners

"The more parents know about what we are doing in the nursery, the more they are able to join in and contribute."

Families from abroad bring with them a wide range of experiences and expectations. In some countries children will not start formal schooling until they are six or seven, while in others they will be expected to read and write at a very early age. Help parents get to grips with pre-school education in Britain by compiling an information booklet about the early years foundation stage.

Teaching tip

Get the information booklet translated into a range of different languages for those parents who cannot read English. Include plenty of photos to help illustrate the meaning of the text.

Parents are their children's first educators and should be kept well informed about what their children are learning within their early years setting. It is especially important to make an extra effort with those families who have only recently arrived in Britain and have little knowledge of the education system. Ensuring they are well informed about the foundation stage curriculum will help them to feel more confident about approaching you with questions and comments about their children's education, and more able to support their children at home.

Compile an information booklet that includes:

- **Key workers:** An explanation of the key worker system.
- **Daily organisation:** An outline of the daily timetable including start times, finish times and lunchtimes, as well as regular daily activities such as circle and story times.
- **Early years curriculum:** How the curriculum is structured, including an overview of the different subject areas and the types of activities and learning experiences you provide to help children learn and develop in each. Include photos of children involved in various activities to illustrate.

Involving parents

Signpost the British Council website, where there is a guide to the UK education system and advice on how parents can support their children, as well as improve their own English (https://eal.britishcouncil.org/parents/schools-uk).

- **The setting:** The layout of your setting, including indoor and outside provision with an explanation of why outdoor learning is so important.
- **Assessment:** How you assess the children's progress, including the use of any baseline testing. The purpose of observations and how these are used to assess the children's progress and plan future learning. The meaning behind terms such as 'early learning goal', 'learning journey' and 'profile'.
- **Approaches to teaching and learning:** An overview of the characteristics of effective learning – playing and exploring, active learning, and creating and thinking critically. An explanation of how young children learn through play.
- **Approaches to teaching literacy:** How reading and writing is taught at your school/setting, when and how you introduce reading books and the reasoning behind these approaches.
- **English as an additional language:** An explanation about why it is so important to support the retention and continued learning of a first language. The strategies in place for helping children who are new to English. Mention the EAL policy (see Idea 2) and explain where to get a copy.
- **Parent help:** An invitation to parents to come in and help out with suggestions for how they can be useful. Include a call-out to parents who can speak particular languages, asking for their help with translating letters and classroom resources, as well as for them to come in and work with small groups of children.

Taking it further

Organise an information morning/evening and invite parents to come in and see what their children have been doing. Deliver a presentation using photos of the children engaged in various activities to explain what learning in the foundation stage looks like. Set out toys and resources for parents to look at and play with, with accompanying short written explanations, in as many languages as possible, about what the children learn while using them.

Parents' room

"We realised that if we wanted parents to work with us we had to make them feel welcome and comfortable to be around us."

Build positive relationships with parents by providing a space where they can meet and socialise with each other as well as practitioners.

Educational experiences and attitudes vary greatly between families from different cultural backgrounds. In some countries parents see education as completely separate from parenting and are intimidated by educators; in others parents welcome the support of educators and are happy to work alongside them. Practitioners in the UK are expected to work closely with parents and so it is a good idea to make an extra effort to make all families feel welcome and comfortable and to demonstrate that you are willing to get to know them and earn their trust and respect. One way of doing this is to open up your doors and welcome them in.

- If you have the space, set up a parents' room with some comfortable seating, a kettle and a supply of tea and coffee.
- Invite parents to use this space at the beginning of each session, and allow them to hang around and chat.
- Plan so that staff can take turns to pop into the room each morning and chat with the parents. Use this opportunity to seek their views on education and what your setting is providing for their children. Find out about their own experiences of schooling and teachers.
- Be respectful and listen to what parents tell you. Demonstrate that you value their opinions and want to work with them.

Multilingual lending library

"It doesn't have to be expensive; we've actually made a lot of the resources ourselves."

Set up a lending library that offers multilingual books and resources that represent the different languages of the children in your setting.

The library should be in an easily accessible area where parents can browse and choose with their children. Provide a signing-out book with space for parents to record the date they borrowed an item, their name and the date they returned it. Stock your library with the following:

- A selection of English and dual-language story and information books. Find both fiction and non-fiction books from Mantra Lingua (uk.mantralingua.com), Bright Books (www.brightbooks.co.uk) and Madeleine Lindley (www.madeleinelindley.com).
- Straightforward games that can be played in any language, for example cards for snap, matching games, picture lotto and jigsaw puzzles.
- Illustrated and laminated nursery rhymes in a variety of languages.
- Hand and finger puppets featuring characters that represent a range of ethnicities.
- Hand-made multilingual board games.
- Hand-made multilingual photo storybooks featuring pictures of the children playing in the setting, participating in special celebrations and out on visits.
- Audio CDs featuring multilingual stories and rhymes.

Ask parents to contribute to the library by making story and rhyme cards in their first languages.

Teaching tip

Put resources in zip-up clear plastic wallets and include laminated multilingual instruction cards with ideas for games and activities to accompany books, stories and rhymes.

Involving parents

BookTrust has produced guidance for parents of children who are learning EAL. Find more information on the website (www.bookstart. org.uk/bookstart-packs/ Bookstart-for-all/dual-languages/tips/).

Reporting back

"We try to keep an open dialogue with parents, which is tricky when they are unable to speak English, but essential nevertheless."

Practitioners are legally obliged to report back to parents during the early years on two occasions: first when a child is aged between two and three years (the two-year progress check), and second in the final term of the reception year (the EYFS profile). In addition, practitioners must maintain ongoing formative assessments and keep parents informed of their children's progress (DfE, 2014).

Involving parents

Make parents feel included and valued by asking for their opinions about their children's progress. Encourage them to share their observations of their children and pass along any significant achievements as well as concerns.

It is good practice to meet regularly with parents and keep them informed of their children's progress. Aim to meet at least once a term with all parents for a 10-minute consultation, bearing in mind that non-English-speaking parents will need longer.

When reporting back to parents of children who speak EAL, Crosse (2007) recommends the following:

- Enlisting the help of a bilingual support assistant or inviting parents to bring along a family member or friend who can translate.
- Ensuring that during the meeting you speak directly to the parents and not the translator. Speak clearly and slowly and pause at regular intervals to give the translator a chance to keep up.
- Using visual aids, such as the children's learning journey or photos from their observation file to help illustrate what you mean.

Magic moments

"Can you do me a magic moment?"

The EYFS Profile Handbook states that 'accurate assessment takes into account a range of perspectives' including those of the children's parents (DfE, 2014). A magic moments display is a non-pressured way of inviting parents to share their children's achievements with you.

All parents are keen to share their children's achievements, and this is a great way to collect their observations of their children on paper so you can include them in the children's learning journeys.

Taking it further

Invite parents to bring in photos of their children doing different activities at home with short written explanations.

- Set up the display in a place that is easily accessible to parents.
- Mount a pocket chart on the wall and place laminated photos of the children in each pocket.
- Fill one pocket with 'magic moment' slips and a pen.
- Write a short explanation inviting parents to take some slips away to fill in, then bring them back and post them in their children's pockets. Explain that the idea is to record their children's achievements at home. A magic moment can be anything, for example good behaviour, counting accurately, reading something or riding a bike.
- Display translations of this explanation in the different languages spoken by parents in the setting. Add that parents can submit their magic moments in any language and are also welcome to pass them along verbally.
- Each day take some time to share any magic moments with all the children in the setting.

Helpful environment

Part 4

On display

"He just loves to press the buttons and listen."

Display is extremely important in the early years, and practitioners put a great deal of effort into producing attractive, colourful and interactive displays that grab the children's attention and give them a sense of pride in their work. Make displays accessible to non-English speakers by including translated headings and captions both in print and as audio recordings.

Teaching tip

Laminate all display headings and captions so that you can use them again. Write the English translation and name of the language on the back of each of the translations before laminating them. Set up a displays concertina file to store everything. Paper-clip English words and phrases to the translations so they are easier to find the next time you need them.

If you have EAL learners in your setting ensure that displays are fully inclusive by translating headings and captions into different languages. It is possible to do this both in print and through the use of audio recordings. There are some fantastic ICT resources around now that can be used to make interactive displays. All of the resources mentioned below are available from TTS (tts-group.co.uk).

- It is helpful to mount wall displays low down so that print is at the children's eye level. If this is not possible, place display headings at the bottom of display boards instead of the top.
- Place written translations next to titles, headings and captions so the children can see their home languages in print. Practitioners can also refer to these and read them out to the children.
- Place Talking Points (buttons that can be attached to wall displays) next to each title, heading and caption. Use these to record translations in the children's home languages so they can press the buttons and listen.
- Hang string across the top or bottom of a display board and peg pictures on to it with Recordable Pegs. Record translated captions for each of the pictures on to the pegs for the children to listen to. These pegs are magnetic so they can also be attached to

Taking it further

Invite children to record their own labels, captions and descriptions on to the different recording devices and include these on the displays.

metallic surfaces without string.

- Set up display tables and place objects inside Rainbow Talking Boxes (boxes that play a recording when opened). Record the name of each object in different languages.
- Place coloured sorting tubs on display tables with matching coloured Talking Points next to them. Record verbal sorting criteria on each of the buttons both in English and other relevant languages.
- Record a question on to a Big Point (larger version of a Talking Point with a removable clear top where you can insert pictures) and place it on a display table. Provide Talking Clipboards with translated recordings of possible answers for the children to listen to and sign their name against whichever they choose.

Label it

"She knows what she wants and can find it without help."

It is important to make the learning environment freely accessible to all children. Sticking picture labels on areas, equipment and resources will help all children, not least those who are learning EAL, to navigate the space and access what they need independently.

Taking it further

Remember that children who are learning EAL will also be learning to recognise their own names like everyone else. Help the children to find their own coat pegs, drawers, drinking bottles, snack cards and self-registration cards by marking them with name labels both in English and their home language, accompanied by photos of their faces. Do the same with group names.

Bonus idea ★

In the early years it is helpful to create a language-rich environment by sticking word labels on objects, for example 'chair', 'table', 'door' and 'whiteboard'. Adapt these to include translations of the words in other relevant languages.

Stick pictorial labels all over the learning environment to help children independently access and replace any resources they want or need. On each label print the word in English together with translations in other relevant languages and an accompanying picture or photograph. Children who are not yet ready to read will be able to look at the pictures, and children who are ready to read will be able to use the pictures as clues to decipher the words. What's more, adults will be able to refer to the translated words and use these to help them speak to each child in their first language.

- Label drawers, cupboards, resource trolleys, storage racks and containers with photos of what they contain.
- Label painting apron pegs with photos of the painting easel and water coverall pegs with photos of the water tray.
- Label toilet doors with male and female person symbols accompanied by a picture of a toilet.
- Remember to label outdoor storage and resources as well.

Pictorial rubrics

"I find these especially useful because they really help new children to become independent more quickly."

Display pictorial rubrics around the setting to help new children who are unfamiliar with routines and expected behaviour.

Ask more confident children in the group if they will help demonstrate routines and examples of good behaviour, so you can take photos and create pictorial rubrics for unfamiliar children to refer to.

- **Toilets:** Take photos of children flushing the toilet, using soap, and rinsing and drying their hands. Add captions, print, laminate them and stick the photos next to the flush, sinks and paper towel dispensers or hand dryers.
- **Snack time:** Take photos of children washing hands, posting their name card, pouring drinks, choosing something to eat, sitting at the table, mopping up a spillage and taking plates and cups to the sink or dishwasher. Create a display in the snack area by mounting the photos with accompanying captions in sequence.
- **Sitting on the carpet:** Take photos of the children sitting still, with legs crossed, facing the front and with hands on laps. Add captions; bottom on the floor, cross legs, face the front, hands on lap.
- **Good listening:** Take photos of children sitting still with hands on laps, looking at the speaker, with one hand to an ear to indicate listening and with a finger to a lip as if thinking. Add captions; 'sit still', 'look at the speaker', 'listen to what is said', 'think about it'.
- **Lining up:** Display photos of the whole group lining up in single file, in pairs and holding hands, and of each key worker group lining up separately. Point to these when asking the children to line up in a particular way.

Teaching tip

Direct eye contact is construed as disrespectful in some cultures. Furthermore, bodily contact and physical gestures may have different meanings. Take this into consideration when creating your rubrics.

Taking it further

Add speech bubbles to the photos containing key words in the target child's home language to help practitioners as they explain routines and behaviours.

Learning the lingo

"I've already got too much to do, let alone learning another language!"

Being faced with the task of learning another language can feel overwhelming for practitioners who speak only English.

Taking it further

Encourage the whole staff to share the responsibility by asking everyone to learn key words and phrases in the different languages of all the children in the setting. Learn songs that are sung on a daily basis in different languages and teach them to the children, and use a multilingual calendar to talk about the date and weather at the beginning of each day.

Practitioners should be forgiven for feeling apprehensive about adding learning another language to their list of responsibilities. However, it is extremely important that children who are learning EAL are supported in their continued use of their first language. Help members of staff who have non-English-speaking children in their key worker groups by doing the following:

- Give key workers additional preparation time so they can collate and learn lists of helpful everyday key words and phrases.
- Use fold-away dividers that can be brought out and opened up for each small group time. Mount displays on the dividers that key workers can refer to: lists of key words such as colours, numbers and shapes; vocabulary linked to the current topic or theme; a list of useful translated phrases such as 'sit in a circle', 'look at me' and 'today we are learning about . . .'; and nursery rhymes and songs in different languages.
- Create lists of key words that relate to topics, themes and areas of learning, and display these around the learning environment for practitioners to refer to. Copy these lists and give them to practitioners to carry around with them on clipboards.

Play the part

"She spends a lot of time in the home corner cooking 'jantar'."

Children learning EAL benefit greatly from first-hand experiences that help them to internalise and process new vocabulary and language. Setting up play experiences will encourage children to practise using their new language and develop it further.

It is a good idea to build on experiences that all children are likely to be able to identify with. This will make EAL learners feel more comfortable, boosting their confidence and encouraging them to talk and interact. Try the following:

- **At home:** Set up a home corner with familiar furniture and household objects, including items that represent a range of cultures.
- **At the park:** Go on a trip to the park. Use the play equipment and have a picnic. Set up a small world play park on a table in the setting and provide a picnic basket containing eating utensils and play food to take outside.
- **At the supermarket:** Visit the local supermarket. Take a shopping list, select the food from the shelves and pay for it. Set up a role-play supermarket indoors and an outdoor market that each stock foods from a range of cultures.
- **On holiday:** Invite children to bring in photos, postcards and scrapbooks from their holidays. Set up role-play aeroplanes, ferries, trains and coaches indoors and outside. Provide luggage and holiday clothing and accessories for the children's pretend travels.
- **On the farm:** Visit a farm where the children can see and name a range of animals and farm machinery. Set up a small world farm indoors and an outdoor role-play farm with ride-on tractor and cuddly toy animals.

Taking it further

Try setting up more exotic play scenarios such as a pirate ship, spacecraft or paleontological dig. Although you will be unable to provide first-hand experience of these they are exciting themes that will appeal to the children's imaginations. Provide context by supplying good-quality information books with large eye-catching pictures and photos. Play with the children and model the use of related language.

Feeling safe and secure

"She's not afraid to have a go, so she's already won most of the battle."

All children will benefit from a positive learning environment where they feel happy to try things out and make mistakes. This is particularly important for children learning EAL, because if they feel worried about making mistakes they will be less likely to have a go at speaking English.

Teaching tip

Foster independence by organising the learning environment so that the children are able to access resources and equipment without help. Allow them the freedom to experiment and try things out without placing restrictions on them, such as disallowing the use of certain resources outside or the mixing up of different sets of toys.

It is important to help young children understand that mistakes are a part of learning. The best way to do this is to create a learning culture in which 'getting it wrong' is valued as a positive learning experience, and those who try are given recognition and praise for their attempts.

- Invest time in creating a supportive learning environment in which everyone is respected and valued. Play community-building games, hold regular circle times, pause to help children work through conflict and help them to empathise with others. Doing this will build children's self-esteem and give EAL learners the confidence to attempt to speak English.
- Support all children's attempts at taking any risks by making time to reflect on what went right and what went wrong. Help children to see the value in failure, and how their experiences can assist them in their next attempts.
- Give EAL learners plenty of praise and reassurance when they have a go at speaking in English, even when they make mistakes. Respond to incorrect vocabulary and phrases by replying with a sentence that uses the correct terminology.

Taking it further

Treat EAL learners as resident experts, and ask them to tell you and other children words for things you come across during play and focused activities in their own languages. Make them proud of their first language.

Time to chill

"Sometimes it seems like it's just a bit too much for her."

Becoming acclimatised to a new country and culture, entering a new learning environment and learning a new language is tiring. When children are starting to zone out or are becoming frustrated, this may be a sign that it is time to take a break.

Take EAL learners into consideration when planning. Set out the learning environment so that it allows these children to take time out every now and again, yet at the same time remain involved in what the rest of the children are doing. Plan activities and set out resources that cover the same theme but require less in terms of language and communication. For example:

- Observational drawing or painting: this can be done independently without the need to talk.
- Multilingual audio CDs: find stories and information books in the children's home languages that they can sit and listen to.
- Jigsaw puzzles: these can be completed alone.
- Playdough: set out themed cutters and mats and leave them to play.
- Dual-language picture books: share these together in a quiet corner.
- Calm and restful space: set this up with cushions and cuddly toys and themed photos, pictures and posters on display. Children can go there to just sit and quietly contemplate.

Taking it further

Help children who are showing signs of frustration by planning activities that will give them the opportunity to vent or burn it off – such as music and dance, running races, climbing trees or rolling out large pieces of paper and throwing paint bombs.

Supporting software

"He loves to go on the computer and so we've been using online games to help him learn English."

There is a vast amount of ICT software available that has been specifically developed to support and enhance EAL teaching and learning.

Suggestions for good-quality software include:

- **Clicker 7** (Crick Software www.cricksoft.com/uk/home.aspx): Use this to create talking books using photos, pictures, animations and videos. Additional software including New to English, Clicker Phonics and Oxford Reading Tree for Clicker can be used for targeted teaching and support, while the Symbol Sets can be used to make communication aids and support early reading.
- **Tizzy's Toybox V2** (Sherston Software shop.sherston.com): Use this to teach the children a range of basic concepts and vocabulary through sorting, matching and sequencing games, as well as early literacy skills through rhyme and sound activities.
- **Purple Mash** (2Simple Software www.2simple.com): This is a website that schools can subscribe to and gain access to a range of software, including open-ended tools and interactive games that can be used to support learning across the curriculum. Use additional add-on 2Start English, where the children enter a virtual multicultural English school to be greeted by pupils who speak 22 different languages.
- **Littlebridge.com** (Little Bridge www.littlebridge.com): This is a website where children can enter a virtual English-speaking world and have a go at a range of activities that aim to improve their English-language skills.

Listening

Part 5

Learning to listen

"It is so important to spend time concentrating on the basics, like being able to listen."

Being able to listen is the first step towards being able to speak. Children learn to speak by listening to the sounds produced by others. Therefore, EAL learners need to be able to listen in order to learn how to speak the English language.

EAL learners may find themselves faced with the task of adapting to an entirely new script and encountering sounds that they have never heard before, as Siraj-Blatchford and Clarke (2000) point out.

- Different languages are accompanied by different non-verbal signals, gestures and facial expressions.
- Conversational language is delivered with the use of slang, repetition, and empty and filled pauses.
- People tend to speak more quickly when in everyday conversation, and frequently interrupt each other.
- Different languages may have different alphabets, symbols and scripts.
- A word or sound may exist in one language but not in another.
- The pronunciation of a letter sound or symbol in one language may be different to another.

Help children develop their listening skills so that they are better equipped to tune in to and pick up English by playing listening games that involve locating sounds, imitating sounds and following instructions (in both English and their first language). Find a good selection of ideas in *The Little Book of Listening* by Clare Beswick (Featherstone Education).

Bonus idea ★

Regular music and movement sessions are helpful for developing listening skills. Provide percussion instruments and drums and encourage the children to imitate, follow and repeat the different rhythms and beats. Plan to regularly sing and clap to songs and rhymes and dance in time to music.

Listening walk

"It's nice to get outside the classroom into the open air and take in the sounds and sights around us."

The most basic listening skill is auditory discrimination, or having the ability to sift out sounds from background noise. This is especially important for children who are learning EAL, because if they can pick out individual sounds they will be better able to hear the sounds of a new language and form these in their own speech.

Listening walks help children to develop their auditory discrimination by asking them to listen out for and home in on individual sounds among background noise.

Taking it further

Take the children out at different times of day as well as for trips off site, where they are likely to hear different sounds and expand their vocabulary further.

- Before leaving think about the different sounds that you are likely to encounter, and print off some pictures that you will be able to use as visual cues. For example car, aeroplane, train, truck, wind symbol, bird, lawnmower, hedge trimmer, church bell, river and emergency vehicles.
- Take the children out for a walk around the local area in small groups so that you will be able to give them all your direct attention.
- Pause every so often and ask everyone to stand still and listen. Ask each child to tell you a sound they can hear. Allow EAL learners to use the picture cards. Encourage them to tell you what they can hear in their first language, and give them the English translation.
- When you get back to the setting ask the children to think back to what they heard. Use the picture cards and revise the vocabulary.

Tuning in

"Estrellita ¿dónde estás?"

In order to hear and learn about how the English language works, EAL learners need to develop a phonological awareness of it, or in other words, an awareness of the sounds, rhythms and patterns of the language. This will help them to develop phonemic awareness, or the ability to identify sounds and letter patterns in English words, which will prepare them for reading and writing.

Children who are able to speak two languages will eventually develop greater phonological awareness. Note, therefore, that it is important to continue to support their language development in their first language rather than concentrating solely on English. Help EAL learners develop their phonological awareness by:

- Creating a peaceful environment with less background noise.
- Planning regular singing and rhyme times both in English and the children's first languages.
- Reading plenty of rhythmical rhyming texts in English to help them become familiar with this new language.
- Organising small group and circle times where children are encouraged to take turns and respond to what each other says, both in English and their first languages.
- Practising active listening by encouraging children to repeat what you have said and tell you what they are going to do in response.
- Sharing stories before re-enacting them with puppets and small world resources, and retelling them with story sequencing cards.

A little concentration . . .

"It would help if he could just concentrate for five minutes!"

Listening involves maintaining attention, concentrating and focusing on what other people say. If children can do this they will be able to retain and process information and respond appropriately. Non-English-speaking children will find this particularly challenging because it takes a great deal of effort. It is therefore very useful to practise concentration skills to help them in this endeavour.

Try playing the following games.

- **Snap, picture lotto, matching pairs and the tray game:** These games not only require focus and concentration, but they can also be used to introduce names of objects and animals. Make your own games to support different themes and topics.
- **Jelly beans:** The children spread out in a large space, listen for you to call out different types of bean and make a movement in response: jelly beans (wobble about), jumping beans (jump), string beans (join hands with others to make a string), broad beans (stand with arms and legs spread wide), baked beans (crouch down into a ball) and runner beans (run around). This game is repetitive and involves actions, which will help EAL learners commit words to memory.
- **Repeat after me:** Sit in a circle and give each child a small drum. Play a short sequence on your drum and ask them to repeat it. Extend the activity by introducing another instrument such as a triangle into the sequence.
- **Simon says:** As well as requiring children to watch and listen, they will be learning the names of body parts and the language to describe simple movements.

Taking it further

Lift-the-flap books are great for fostering good concentration and improving memory. Revisit these books with EAL learners on a regular basis and ask them to tell you what is under each flap. This will encourage them to focus as well as help them to pick up new vocabulary. The *Spot* books by Eric Hill (Puffin) are particularly good for this because there is a large selection covering numerous themes.

Rhythm and rhyme

"Rhyme time is one of the children's favourite times of day. Everyone joins in – even those who do not fully understand what we are singing about!"

Every language has its own phonology, and children who are learning to speak English need plenty of opportunities to become familiar with the sounds and rhythms of the language (Palmer and Bayley, 2013).

Teaching tip

Try introducing a 'song/rhyme of the week'. Repeat it a couple of times a day to give the children a chance to learn it properly, and revisit them each week. This repetition will help children who are learning EAL to commit the songs and rhymes to memory, and will give them the confidence to join in.

Taking it further

Use songs and rhymes throughout the day to help with transitions and routines. Sing hello, weather and days of the week songs in the mornings, sing a tidy-up song at the end of each session and sing a goodbye song at the end of each day.

An important part of early language development is building phonological awareness (an awareness of the sounds in language). All young children need to play with language in order to develop this, and one of the most effective ways is through regular exposure to rhythmical, rhyming texts and songs with repeated refrains.

- Rhythmical, rhyming texts will help children become familiar with the sounds, rhythms and patterns of spoken English.
- Reciting rhymes, singing songs, rapping and repeating chants will help to increase children's fluency of speech.
- Most children enjoy singing and respond well to musical activities, which will encourage less confident and shy children to join in.
- Providing instruments and playing clapping games will help children hear the rhythms and beats in words and sentences.
- Singing and rapping helps to improve articulation and speech, as well as children's control over pitch and volume.
- Songs and rhymes with actions are especially helpful for EAL learners because of the visual aspect.

Keep it simple

"It's drummed into you to use lots of language all the time. Children with EAL don't need that; it's best to keep it simple."

When teaching children who are learning EAL it is tempting to expose them to a continuous flow of spoken language in an attempt to get them speaking and understanding English as soon as possible. However, this can be counterproductive.

A bombardment of English words and phrases will confuse children who are new to the language. As a consequence it is possible that they will either switch off or become exhausted from trying so hard to concentrate and work out your meaning. Introduce new words and phrases slowly with plenty of pauses to give children a chance to think and speak as well.

- When joining in the children's play, watch them for cues to figure out what they are interested in and use this as a springboard for introducing topical vocabulary.
- Try not to speak out of context. Stay on topic to avoid confusion, and take time to repeat words and phrases to help the children absorb them.
- Repeat and add to what the children say to consolidate their learning as well as gradually extend their vocabulary and understanding. For example, if a child says 'Look, big tower', you could say, 'Yes, it is a big tall tower', while demonstrating your meaning by indicating height with your hands.
- Speak slowly and point to objects and pictures to give visual clues.
- Ensure that you encourage children to use their first language alongside English. Give them time to speak in whichever language they choose, and if that is their own language offer the English translation.

Teaching tip

It is not unusual for children who are learning English to form sentences using the grammatical conventions of their first language, resulting in utterances that do not altogether make sense. Help these children by acknowledging what they say, while repeating the sentence using the correct grammar and word order.

Speaking

Part 6

Give me a sign

"We use Makaton with some of our children who have communication and language difficulties. It never occurred to me that it would be helpful to EAL learners!"

Use a sign support system alongside spoken language to help convey meaning.

Involving parents

Give the parents a copy of the core signs and symbols that you are using with their child so they can use them at home.

One technique for helping children who are learning EAL understand your meaning is to use non-verbal cues and signals. Sign support systems such as Makaton (www.makaton.org) and Signalong (www.signalong.org.uk) offer a broader selection of non-verbal signs. Children can read these visual cues to help them translate spoken English, and use them alongside their home language to deliver meaning to others until they are able to remember and recall the English terms.

- Use signs throughout daily routines and when singing rhymes and songs. Regular use will not only consolidate your own knowledge of the signs but will help all the children in the group to pick them up and remember them. They will then be able to use them to communicate with those children who are new to English.
- Continue to talk when using a sign support system. Sign support systems are just what they say they are – systems that are intended to support the use of spoken language. They are not intended to replace speech but should be used in conjunction with it.
- Include pictures of signs and symbols on labelling and displays to refer to and copy when talking with children who are new to English.
- Add signs and symbols from your chosen sign support system to survival language cue cards and fans (see Idea 6) for both children and practitioners to refer to and learn.

Time to talk

"He knew the cocoon was fake and surprised us by coming out with words like 'diamond' and 'tissue' as he tried to convince the others."

Before EAL learners can be expected to read and write they need to be able to understand English word meanings, and this language comprehension comes from speaking and listening.

When children play together they develop and extend each others' language and vocabulary. Give the children in your setting plenty of time and space to talk. Set up provocations and activities that grab their interest and get them chatting, discussing and arguing with each other.

- Place unusual objects in random places around the setting for the children to discover, examine and wonder about.
- Display questions in the different areas of the learning environment for the children to seek answers to. Use questions such as 'What might happen if . . .?', 'Where do you think this came from?', 'How do you think this happened?' or 'Have you ever wondered . . .?'
- Fill the art and design area with a range of good-quality craft and junk modelling supplies, and try to provide enough space so the children are able to construct and create in pairs and groups.
- Place a puppet in trouble and leave it for the children to discover and help. Try putting the puppet on a low roof, up a tree, jammed in a window or clinging to the top of a climbing frame.
- Print footprints on the floor of the outdoor area leading to an open window and then through the inside. Upturn tables and tip over toys to make it look as if something very large has wandered through the setting.

Teaching tip

Remember to take a step back and allow the children to play and talk without adult interference. When children play together they use language they might not use with an adult. Children who are learning EAL need this valuable experience; it will help them develop conversational language that will enable them to communicate better with their friends and peers.

A tip from Vygotsky

"We often just play alongside the children and chat to ourselves. Before you know it, they are chatting along with you."

Siraj-Blatchford and Clarke (2000) highlight the link between Vygotsky's theory of the zone of proximal development and learning an additional language.

Teaching tip

Rather than drawing attention to mistakes, simply repeat words and phrases using the correct words and pronunciations, and move on. Give children plenty of recognition and praise for attempting to use and understand English.

Early years pioneer Lev Vygotsky (1896–1934) believed that children's learning is extended by the assistance of more knowledgeable others. Educational psychologist Jerome Bruner (1915–) agreed, and introduced the term 'scaffolding' to describe this process. Help children develop their spoken English with the following strategies:

- **Using self-speech:** Talking to yourself as you play.
- **Using parallel talk:** Talking about what a child is doing as they play.
- **Re-phrasing:** Responding to a child by repeating what they say using the correct phrasing and pronunciation.
- **Grouping:** Putting children in groups where they can observe and listen to their peers.
- **Demonstrating:** Using physical gestures and actions to help demonstrate meaning.
- **Describing:** Adding description to sentences, for example, 'Can you put your nice yellow coat on, please?'
- **Modelling:** Teaching new vocabulary through natural conversation during play.
- **Leading:** Beginning a sentence and pausing so that a child can complete it.
- **Echoing:** Encouraging children to repeat words and simple phrases, for example while sharing a picture book.
- **Waiting:** Giving children time to think and respond.
- **Extending:** Building on what children say by repeating their sentence and adding a bit more.

Taking it further

Work with children who are learning EAL in small groups. That way you can give them your full attention so they will find it easier to follow what is going on and have plenty of chances to speak.

Block play

"We find that children become very involved in building with blocks and play for long periods together. They might not be able to speak the same language but they seem to understand each other all the same."

'Children creating with blocks are representing ideas as well. Learners need to express themselves in concrete ways before progressing to abstract methods. Through block play, children build a foundation for future literacy.' (Huleatt, 2013)

The great thing about block play is its open-ended nature. Children can create pretty much anything their imagination allows. They can build large constructions using hollow blocks, planks and crates, and small world scenes using solid unit blocks. They can make buses, boats and trains or stepping stones, caves and castles.

Block play inspires children to overcome language barriers and play together with shared creativity and imagination. It does not matter whether they share a common language or not; the blocks will motivate them to play side by side, communicating with each other in their respective languages and using physical gestures to get their meanings and ideas across.

Join the children as they play.

- Ask them about what they have constructed. Allow them to point out the different features of their design and explain it in their own language. Ensure that English-speaking children give their non-English-speaking peers a chance to respond.
- Model the use of positional language, for example 'on top', 'beside', 'next to' and 'under'.
- Talk about how 'tall', 'short', 'long', 'narrow' or 'wide' a construction is.
- Examine the different blocks, name their shapes and describe their features.

Taking it further

Provide additional resources such as small world people, vehicles and animals to enhance and extend the play and promote further language development.

61

Board games

"No, no, look see . . . I go up the ladder."

Use board games to practise memory and concentrations skills, as well as to introduce and reinforce vocabulary learning and to encourage EAL learners to speak.

Taking it further

Make your own board games that aim to teach certain vocabulary or practise particular skills. Search online for printable templates or go to the Twinkl website (www.twinkl.co.uk) or *Times Educational Supplement* resources website (www.tes.co.uk/teaching-resources) for ready-made games.

Choose games designed specifically for young children, with bright colourful pictures. Following are some suggestions for games that are useful for working with EAL learners.

- **Shopping List** (www.orchardtoys.com): This game encourages children to focus and concentrate, and introduces food and supermarket vocabulary. Also available are fruit and veg and clothes booster packs.
- ***The Gruffalo* and *The Very Hungry Caterpillar* memory games** (see online resources for Amazon links to these): Use these to repeat and reinforce vocabulary learning and practise memory skills.
- **Giant Snakes and Ladders** (www.hope-education.co.uk): Play this game to practise counting, recognising and naming numbers and to practise the use of positional and directional language. Turn taking games like this will also encourage children to talk to each other as they discuss the rules and negotiate game play.
- **Story By Pictures Puzzles** (www.earlyyearsresources.co.uk): Use these picture sequencing puzzles to introduce English vocabulary and routine phrases related to familiar themes such as baking, going to school, shopping, waking up and going to bed.
- **Everyday Life Bingo** (www.eduzone.co.uk): This simple picture lotto game can be used to introduce vocabulary and as a springboard for conversation that will further develop language and comprehension.

Dinosaur discovery

"He ran to the wall and just stared at the enormous silhouette of the diplodocus. It was great; he was absolutely captivated."

Provide the inspiration that EAL learners need to speak and use new language and vocabulary by setting up a dinosaur-themed discovery centre.

Set up the following provocations that will appeal to the children's senses and get them thinking and talking.

- Cut out dinosaur shapes from black sugar paper, place them on an overhead projector and project the enlarged silhouettes on the wall.
- Set up a light box and cover it in green cellophane. Add some strips of green ribbon, green glass pebbles and green wool and place some small toy dinosaurs on top.
- Fill a deep tray with green slime. Add some rocks, leaves and toy dinosaurs.
- Press the feet of very big toy dinosaurs into large slabs of modelling clay, pour over some plaster of Paris and leave it to set. Peel off the modelling clay to reveal some fossilised footprints for the children to examine.
- Bury dinosaur bones in a sand tray and provide small tools and brushes so the children can excavate them.
- Place a selection of real fossils, snakeskins that have been shed and responsibly sourced reptile skin for the children to touch and examine.
- Cut pteranodon shapes out of cardboard, cover them in aluminium foil and hang them from the ceiling. Turn the lights down and give the children torches to shine on them.
- Set out a range of information books about dinosaurs with large bright pictures, such as *The Big Book of Big Dinosaurs* by Alex Frith (Usborne).

Teaching tip

As the children explore and play with each of the resources and activities, observe and introduce vocabulary to describe what they can see, hear, smell and feel. Prepare vocabulary lists in different languages beforehand so you can offer these in the children's first languages.

Taking it further

Read *Dinosaur Roar!* by Henrietta and Paul Stickland (Doubleday). This simple picture book is great for introducing opposites to children who are new to English. It has very simple text with accompanying pictures that clearly illustrate meaning.

Spots and stripes

"We make it hot and colour come off."

Enthuse the children and inspire them to talk by using creative methods that will interest and excite them.

This activity is especially good for children who are learning EAL because it involves three different stages. The children complete a series of short activities that introduce a number of artistic techniques, and at the same time they are introduced to a range of vocabulary in short bursts that is revised with each stage.

Stage one

- Begin by looking in some information books that feature large, good-quality pictures of wild animals. Point out different creatures and see if the children can name them in either their first language or English. Look at the creatures' individual features, and in particular their colouring and patterns. Introduce vocabulary such as 'legs', 'tail', 'ears', 'fur', 'scales', 'spots' and 'stripes'.

- Provide sugar paper and poster paints for the children to paint a picture of a wild animal. Guide them to look at the pictures of the animals in the books and choose their colours carefully. Introduce terms such as 'paint', 'brush' and 'colour'. Name the different colours, experiment with mixing and talk about what happens.

- Leave the paintings to dry.

Stage two

- Give the children each a piece of white paper and a selection of fabric crayons. Ask them to colour the paper in the same pattern as their animal painting. Take the opportunity to repeat the vocabulary associated with colour and pattern that you introduced in the first stage.

Stage three

- Set up an ironing board in a safe place where you can use it without any danger of the children coming into contact with the iron.
- Bring the children to the ironing board and show them the iron. Ask them if they know what an iron is used for and how it works. Introduce vocabulary such as 'danger', 'hot', 'burn', 'iron', 'clothing' and 'crease'.
- Place one of the pieces of paper with a fabric crayon pattern face down on a piece of white cotton fabric. Fold the fabric over the paper to prevent it from burning, then run the hot iron over it several times.
- Peel the paper off the fabric to reveal a copy of the pattern. Hold it up to show the children and explain what has happened, using vocabulary such as 'hot', 'press', 'melt', 'crayon', 'transfer' and 'stick'.
- Once all the patterns have been ironed and transferred, look at them in turn and talk about the colours and patterns again.

Stage four

- Use pinking shears to cut out the fabric patterns.
- Cut out a section from the middle of each of the children's painted animals and stick their fabric pattern in the empty space.
- Display the animals and label them in different languages.
- Invite parents in to look at the display and encourage the children to explain to their parents how they make their pictures in whichever language they choose.

It's a small world

"I don't suppose 'dragon' is all that common a word, but she loved playing with the castle and it got her talking with the other children."

Although it helps to build on familiar concepts and experiences when teaching children a new language, it is just as important to think of ways to excite, interest and inspire EAL learners to interact with their peers.

Taking it further

Other small world scenes include outer space, dinosaur land, knights and princesses, pirate island, under the sea, fairy tales and superheroes. Find a selection of good-quality resources at Early Excellence (www.earlyexcellence. com), Essentials for Education (www. essentialsforeducation. co.uk) and the Early Learning Centre (www. elc.co.uk).

Put a little imagination into small world scenes with the use of a combination of natural materials, purpose-made props and character pieces.

- **Tuff Spot:** This is a popular resource in the early years because it is a good shape and size for small world play. The Tuff Spot is available in a range of colours, it is possible to buy a stand to raise it off the floor and there is a wide selection of accompanying scene mats available for creating backgrounds to small world scenes. Cosy supplies a good range (www.cosydirect.com).
- **Fairy land:** Create this scene using pieces of bark, moss, pot plants and flowers, coloured glass pebbles, wooden toadstools, terracotta plant pots, coloured cellophane, glitter and toy fairies. Again, Cosy has a large selection of fairy garden resources.
- **Land of the dragons:** Place a selection of dark-coloured jagged rocks on the tray with sand and small stones. Make a cave out of plaster of Paris and paint it grey, put some gold, jewels and gems inside then add some dragons. Yellow Door has produced a dragon realm scene kit (www.yellow-door.net).
- **Arctic ice:** Line the tray with fake snow, sprinkle on some glitter, add clear glass pebbles, clear Perspex rocks, shredded blue cellophane, a small shallow tray containing frozen water, and toy arctic animals and explorers. Again, find an arctic scene kit in the Yellow Door catalogue.

Going live

"He doesn't speak much to us, but when he gets up on that stage he sings and shouts all afternoon!"

Encourage EAL learners to lose their inhibitions by setting up a stage in the outside area.

Although some EAL learners may not speak much during small group focus tasks with adults, they may nevertheless enjoy play that involves singing, dancing and performing. Exploit this interest and spur them on by setting up a stage and providing a variety of props and costumes. In addition, tempt those children who are less confident by giving them interesting equipment such as voice changers and microphones that they can experiment with.

- Set up a temporary stage using upturned crates covered with a sheet of wood. Otherwise, use playground chalk to mark out a stage area on the floor. Arrange chairs and benches in front of it.
- Set up a backstage area with dressing-up clothes, puppets, large picture books, musical instruments and a box of open-ended resources that the children can use to improvise with.
- Set up a CD player with a selection of multicultural music and multilingual story CDs for the children to choose from.
- Find voice changers and microphones from educational suppliers including TTS (www.tts-group.co.uk) and Early Years Resources (www.earlyyearsresources.co.uk).

> **Bonus idea** ★
>
> Invite a professional storyteller in to perform some stories and songs for the children. Find out about multicultural theatre companies in your area and hire them to come in and give a performance both for the children and their parents.

This is how I feel

"She would get frustrated and bite other children when they could not understand what she was trying to say."

The importance of personal, social and emotional development is recognised within the EYFS, where it is identified as a prime area of learning. A main priority when working those learning EAL, should be to help them express their own feelings as early as possible.

Children who are able to understand and express their own feelings as well as empathise with the feelings of others will develop into self-confident individuals who are able to make a positive contribution to society. It is important to ensure that children who are learning EAL are able to express themselves clearly to others in order to avoid them becoming frustrated.

- Create a feelings display with pictures of facial expressions depicting various feelings with labels in English and other languages.
- Use persona dolls and puppets to role-play common PSED scenarios that occur in the setting, for example with regard to sharing, taking turns, hurting others and excluding other children. Demonstrate the feelings of the puppets through their verbal tone and body language. Use your facial expressions and verbal tone to convey how you feel about their behaviour.
- Hold a daily check-in each morning, where each child can tell you how they are feeling that day. Sit in a circle and greet each other with a 'Good morning' followed by 'I am feeling . . .'. Take time to acknowledge the children's responses and talk through their feelings.
- Teach children learning EAL key words and visual aids that they can use to express their feelings when playing with others. A colour-coded fan featuring pictures of faces conveying different feelings can help them tell you and other children how they feel.

Puppet talk

"We have a character called Claude in our classroom and the children talk to him all the time and include him in their play. We usually use him for group times and whole-class teaching and get him to ask questions. Some children talk more to him than to us."

Young children respond really well to puppets and persona dolls. They really are great way of capturing the children's interest and getting them thinking and talking, and can be used to introduce language associated with everyday life.

Introduce some large character puppets to the setting and treat them as part of the group. Sit them at tables to play games, include them in circle times and use them to help during group times. Once they are fully established take the puppets out and photograph them engaged in everyday activities. Some ideas include:

- Sitting on buses, boats and trains
- Shopping at the supermarket
- Playing at the park
- Eating a picnic lunch
- Having dinner at a restaurant
- Doing some housework
- On a bike ride

Explain that your puppet has taken some photos of what it was up to at the weekend. Show the photos to the children and ask the children to suggest where the puppet went, who it was with and what it did.

Teaching tip

When setting up your photos make your puppets stand/sit up by sliding bamboo sticks inside their clothing. Also position arms, legs and heads with the help of catgut tied to furniture, fencing and trees.

Taking it further

Take photos of puppets in a variety of predicaments to open up discussion about risk and safety – for example playing on a building site, climbing a tree, swinging on a gate or stuck on a roof.

Bonus idea

Send the puppet home with children over the weekends along with a cheap camera and notebook. Ask parents to help their children write a diary entry about what they all got up to.

Understanding

Part 7

Deeper understanding

"I think she's getting confused because she's learning too many languages at once."

Conteh (2012) explains that multilingual children develop a deeper understanding of how language works and are more flexible in their use of language. She points out that this knowledge is transferable and that multilingual children are likely to become more creative and critical thinkers in the long run.

Involving parents

It is not unusual for some parents to discontinue the use of the first language at home and concentrate solely on English. Work with these parents to help them understand the benefits of learning two languages for their children's overall development, and explain that although it may appear to delay their children at first, it will have tremendous benefits for the future.

One of the main objectives in the early years foundation stage is to help young children gain an understanding of the world around them by planning hands-on learning experiences that are supported by high-quality verbal interactions and conversations. Bilingual children will develop a greater knowledge and understanding if they are able to process information in both languages. Consider the following:

- Because children use language to process information, those who are new to English will have a bank of knowledge and experience that has already been internalised in their first language. This is the foundation on which their future learning is to be based, and so practitioners need to acknowledge and build on this. Help children who are learning EAL by introducing new concepts in their first language to ensure they have a secure understanding before explaining them in English.
- Try to employ bilingual support staff to ensure the continued development of children's first languages alongside English. If this is not possible, seek assistance from parents or outside agencies who can help you collate lists of key words and phrases that relate to topics, themes and areas of learning.

Visual aids

"I often catch him fiddling with his shoes during carpet time, and I struggle to keep his attention."

Use physical gestures, real objects, props, pictures and puppets as visual aids to capture the children's attention and keep them interested and engaged.

Listening and understanding involves decoding sounds to ascertain meaning. Children who speak EAL can take several seconds to process a spoken word, which makes listening and maintaining attention hard work. The use of visual aids can make a huge difference in terms of how much these children are able to take in and understand.

- Use physical gestures and exaggerated facial expressions during explanations and stories.
- Take time to give visual demonstrations of activities, holding up and naming equipment and resources.
- Use laminated photos and picture cards when introducing new topics and vocabulary.
- Download emotion cards featuring facial expressions that convey different feelings. Alternatively take photos of the children in your setting, demonstrating the different facial expressions. Use these during morning check-in and circle time (see Idea 54).
- Use character puppets and props when reading and telling stories. Find printable stick puppets for popular picture books on teaching resource websites. In addition, The Puppet Company (uk.thepuppetcompany. com) has produced a range of finger puppets for traditional tales and nursery rhymes.

Bonus idea ★

Story bags are a great resource for storytelling, and there is a wide selection on the market. They typically contain a well-known picture book along with props, characters, games, books, cuddly toys and jigsaws to accompany the story. Storysack (www.storysack.com) has produced a range of story bags aimed specifically at children who speak EAL.

You teach me

"The children absolutely love this game. They think it's hilarious when I get it wrong, and love to tell me what I should have said."

Boost children's self-esteem and motivation to learn by asking them to teach you their first language.

Invite the children to help you make a set of flash cards for each new theme or topic, and use them to play a simple game that will teach them English words, while they teach you the words in their first languages.

- Help the children to cut out pictures printed from the Internet or from magazines, and stick them on to cards.
- Tell the children the English word for each picture and ask them to tell you what it is in their first language.
- Type and print the words in each relevant language and stick them on to the back of the picture cards.
- Laminate the cards for game play.
- Play the game: Lay out the cards with the pictures facing up. Take turns to pick a card and say what the picture is without looking at the words on the back. EAL learners should try to remember the words in English, and you should try to remember them in the children's first languages. Each time a player gets a word right they get to keep the card. If they get the word wrong it stays on the table until it is picked up by another player. The game is finished when all the cards are gone.

Captured on film

"We often take video recordings of children who can't speak a lot of English because we can use them to go over and revise activities later on."

Repetition is vital for children who are learning EAL. Photos and film make it possible to revisit and reflect on learning experiences as well as revise and extend the associated language and vocabulary.

One option is to take photos of the children as they play or take part in a guided activity, and use the photos to create a book or display that will aid reflection.

- **Book:** Paste the photos into a book and add speech bubbles and captions featuring comments the children made throughout the activity.
- **Display:** Mount the photos on to a low-level display with captions and question prompts.

Share the book or visit the display to look at the photos and talk through the activity. Repeat key vocabulary and encourage the children to add their own comments.

Another option is to film the children.

- Play back the recording and pause every now and again to make comments and repeat key words and phrases. Give the children a chance to point things out and speak if they wish.
- Play the recording again, this time without any volume, to give the children an opportunity to add their own commentary.

Teaching tip

Children love to look at photos of themselves and watch themselves on film. Therefore, this is best done with individuals or small groups so that EAL learners do not get drowned out in the excitement and have a chance to listen and speak.

A good question

"She fades out during our whole-group discussions because she can't keep up with the questioning."

The Every Child a Talker guidance recommends that when working with EAL learners 'modelling language and using descriptive commentary should make up about 80% of your interactions and no more than 20% should be direct questioning' (DCSF, 2009a). However, questions are a vital part of early education and so should not be avoided altogether.

Taking it further

Remember, just because a child cannot speak English it does not mean they are incapable of more complex thought. Employ the help of a bilingual assistant to ask open questions that will stretch more able children and get them using higher-order thinking skills such as analysing, relating to experience and offering opinions in their first language.

When directing questions in English at EAL learners, consider the following:

- Closed questions are simpler to understand and are helpful for focusing children and guiding discussion. They are particularly useful for directing at those children who need a confidence boost but are only able to formulate short answers.
- Initially it is helpful to use questions that ask children to name, label and describe because they require straightforward responses.
- Questions can be used as a way to introduce vocabulary through offering alternatives, for example 'Would you like a fork or a spoon?' or 'Would you like to play inside or outside?' Accompanying questions with physical gestures will help to convey meaning.
- Do not ask too many questions in succession. Give the children thinking time to formulate a response and praise any attempts at answering.
- Divide children into talk partners, and if possible pair up children who speak the same language. This gives them a chance to learn from each other and to discuss the answer in their home language before attempting it in English and sharing it with the rest of the group.

Sort it out

"We teach EAL learners using the same kinds of activities that we use with all young children who are learning to talk."

Research shows that activities involving comparing and classifying objects help children to acquire new words more quickly (Frost, et al., 2015).

Sorting activities that require children to compare objects help them to categorise according to purpose and appearance. They also introduce children to a wide variety of descriptive terms and vocabulary. Use these games with children who are learning EAL to help them link key concepts in their own language with English.

Teaching tip

Frost, *et al.* (2015) advocate keeping these games simple so as not to overwhelm children with choices and make the learning more difficult. Only give them a small number of objects to sort, and introduce just one or two new items at a time.

- **Whatever the weather:** Print and laminate three different weather symbols such as a raincloud, sun and snowflake. Fill a box with a selection of clothing items suited to different weathers, for example, coats/anoraks, hats/caps, shoes/boots, shorts/trousers and t-shirts/jumpers. Ask the children to sort the clothing to suit each type of weather.
- **Beanbag dash:** Spread four different-coloured beanbags across the floor of a wide-open space. Place four coloured hoops in the corners of the space. Allocate a colour to each child, and challenge them to grab the beanbags and drop them in the matching-coloured hoops.
- **Beading:** Provide the children with laces and beads. Demonstrate sorting the beads according to colour and shape, then spend some time making necklaces and describing patterns.
- **Vehicle play:** Set up a garage and fill it with vehicles. Challenge the children to park the vehicles in colour groups or according to type. Take the opportunity to count and compare the number of vehicles in each category.

Jeden, dwa, trzy

"He can count to 20 in his own language already, so I know I need to build on this."

Help children who are learning EAL develop a sense of number by introducing early numerical concepts in their first language.

Taking it further

Support children's early mathematical mark making by providing them with clipboards, notepads and playground chalks so they can record their mathematical thinking whenever and wherever. You can support children learning EAL by displaying numbers in a variety of scripts so they can see them represented in their own languages.

Young children need to have a secure knowledge of number before they can move on in their mathematical learning. This means being able to recite numbers in order, count, quantify, compare and recognise numbers. In order to ensure that children learning EAL develop a good basic understanding it helps to use numbers in their first language.

- Make number cards and number lines that feature number names in a variety of different languages. On each card print the number in the centre with the written words above and below in English and the alternative language.
- Create number and counting displays in different scripts.
- Collate a selection of multilingual number rhymes to sing with all the children in the group, as well as during small group time.
- Put together some multilingual number bags. Stick a number on the outside of the bag and fill it with number cards featuring different languages, counting objects and pictures.
- Source dual-language counting books. Little Linguist supplies these in a wide selection of languages (www.little-linguist.co.uk).
- Share picture books featuring number and counting rhymes from a variety of cultures. These books expose children to rhythmical rhyming language while teaching numbers in English. Examples include, *We All Went on Safari* by Laurie Krebs and Julia Cairns (Barefoot Books) and *Engines* by Lisa Bruce and Stephen Waterhouse (Bloomsbury).

Playdough

"You want a cake? They strawberry."

Playdough is very popular, especially with younger children, and offers many opportunities for language and vocabulary development.

Make your own playdough by pouring two cups of flour into a large saucepan with one cup of salt and one cup of water. Add a few drops of food colouring, two tablespoons of sunflower oil and four tablespoons of cream of tartar. Gently warm while mixing with a wooden spoon. When the dough comes together knead it for a couple of minutes. Join children as they play with the dough, and introduce nouns and verbs that describe what they are doing.

- Provide themed shape cutters to introduce the children to a variety of nouns such as words for animals, vehicles and shapes.
- Make different-coloured dough and ask the children to name the colours in their own language, while you offer the English translation.
- Talk about how the dough feels and what happens when you try to 'mould', 'flatten', 'roll', 'cut', 'squash' and 'shape' it.
- Add various food essences, describe the smell and talk about associated foods.
- Add different-coloured glitter to different-coloured doughs and talk about how they look, introducing vocabulary such as 'shine', 'sparkle', 'glitter' and 'twinkle'.
- Provide patterned rollers, printers, wheels and extruders and talk about how the dough behaves and looks when you 'mould' it, 'squeeze' it, 'print' it and 'roll' it.
- Provide baking equipment such as rolling pins, pastry cutters and cupcake tins, and use these to introduce language associated with cooking and food.

Bonus idea ★

Make playdough mats that fit with different topics and themes. For example, make shape mats with pictures of circles, squares, rectangles, stars, diamonds and triangles labelled in different languages, and provide shape cutters.

Making minibeasts

"It ladybird and it got spots."

Make these minibeasts and help children build a bank of vocabulary about living things while also learning some language associated with art and design.

Craft activities like this provide the context children learning EAL need in order to process and remember new language and vocabulary.

- Begin by observing real minibeasts outside, then looking in some information books that feature large, good-quality pictures. Point out different creatures and see if the children can name them in either their first language or English. Look at the creatures' individual features, and name and count the different body parts.
- Invite the children to point out which minibeast they would like to make.
- Give them a lump of self-hardening clay each and ask them to mould it into the body shape of their chosen creature. Take some time to describe the shapes they are creating.
- Provide pipe cleaners, wobbly eyes, small beads and gems for the children to add features to their creatures. Show them how to stick the objects into the clay to create features and patterns, and how to bend the pipe cleaners to create the shapes of legs and wings. Name and count the different body parts.
- Leave the clay to dry.
- Examine the dry models and talk about what has happened, introducing words such as 'wet', 'dry', 'soft' and 'hard'.
- Give the children some poster paint and small brushes to add more colour and detail.

Happy birthday!

"We've learned to sing 'Happy Birthday' in five different languages!"

Everyone has a birthday, making it possible to start a tradition of celebrating each birthday with the same routine while regularly revising the associated vocabulary.

Birthdays can be used to inspire a range of activities and teach language linked to time, celebration, tradition and baking.

- **Birthday display:** Create a display featuring 12 objects, for example, birthday cakes, balloons or a train with 12 carriages. Label the objects so they represent the months of the year in different languages. Stick named photos of the children on the months in which their birthdays fall and write the actual date. At the beginning of each month go to the display and read out the months of the year in sequence. Stop on the current month and point out if anyone's birthday is coming up.
- **Make birthday cakes:** Bake birthday fairy cakes with small groups. Name the ingredients, talk through the process and name colours, shapes and patterns when decorating them later.
- **Sing together:** Sing 'Happy Birthday' in different languages when handing out the cakes.
- **Read together:** Share some books about birthday celebrations such as *Postman Bear* by Julia Donaldson (Macmillan), and *Birthdays Around the World* by Jay Dale (Raintree). Ask the children about their own experiences of celebrating birthdays at home with their families.
- **Role-play:** Provide toy birthday cakes with candles for the children to hold pretend celebrations during play.

Teaching tip

Be sensitive to the feelings of children who do not celebrate birthdays, for example Jehovah's Witnesses. Speak with parents and ask them how they feel about their children being involved in birthday celebrations and if there is anything else special you can do with them instead.

Involving parents

Ask parents about any cultural traditions and related songs, objects or symbols that represent birthday celebrations in their country of origin.

81

The Gingerbread Man

"Run, run as fast as you can! You can't catch me, I'm the Gingerbread Man!"

The Gingerbread Man is a good example of how traditional tales present a wealth of opportunities for English language development across all areas of learning.

Use traditional tales to provide the context that EAL learners need in order to extend their language and vocabulary. For example, a topic based around the story of the Gingerbread Man can be used to teach English in the following ways.

Communication and language

- Read the story to the children in big book format and point to the pictures as you read to indicate meaning.
- Prompt the children to join in with the repeated refrains. Get EAL learners excited and wanting to join in. The Gingerbread Man is running away and shouting over his shoulder. Encourage the children to do the same.
- Share alternative multicultural versions of the story, such as *The Runaway Chapatti* by Susan and Adam Price. (Although this book is now out of print there are second-hand editions available online. Otherwise find an electronic version on the *Times Educational Supplement* resources website: www.tes. co.uk/teaching-resource/the-runaway-chapati-6293441.)

Personal, social and emotional development

- The story explores issues around being boastful and being wary of strangers. Involve the children in re-enacting the story with puppets and props to help them consider the consequences of the Gingerbread Man's actions.
- As you speak the Gingerbread Man's part, use exaggerated facial expressions and your tone of voice to portray his emotions, including

happiness, excitement, boastfulness, cockiness and fear.

Physical development

- Go outside and run like the Gingerbread Man. Get the children to take on the roles of the different characters that chase the Gingerbread Man throughout the book, and encourage them to recite the main repetitive phrases from the story.

Literacy

- Read dual-language versions of the story. If you cannot find any make some yourself with the help of parents and support assistants.
- Create story cards and ask the children to sequence the main events. Encourage them to retell the story in their own words in whichever language they choose.
- Make up alternative endings. Ask the children 'What if the Gingerbread Man came across a . . .?' Show EAL learners pictures of different animals as prompts.

Mathematical development

- Use buttons on gingerbread people for counting activities.
- Make different-sized gingerbread people out of real gingerbread or playdough.

Understanding the world

- Make gingerbread biscuits. Talk about the ingredients, name the baking equipment, weigh out the amounts needed, describe the preparation and baking process, describe the shapes of the biscuits and explain what is happening in the oven. Create key word lists in the relevant languages beforehand and refer to these as you talk about the different aspects involved.

Expressive arts and design

- Provide clay for the children to make non-perishable gingerbread people. Explore and describe the properties of clay. Name body parts and facial features. Supply a choice of paint and talk about the patterns and colours the children create.

> **Bonus idea** ★
>
> Use different traditional tales to introduce language surrounding other themes: explore number and size through Goldilocks and the Three Bears; investigate the weather using Aesop's fable The Sun and the Wind as inspiration; learn about healthy eating with Hansel and Gretel; go out into the woods like Little Red Riding Hood.

Reading and writing

Part 8

In context

"She is really good at blending, but doesn't really understand what she's reading."

EAL learners are just as capable of practising and using synthetic phonics as their English-speaking peers (DCSF, 2009b). Some may already have experience of synthetic phonics from learning to read in their country of origin. However, although these children may be able to decode English words, they might not understand their meaning.

Teaching tip

Children learning EAL are also capable of memorising sight words and should be encouraged to do so like their English-speaking peers (DCSF, 2009b). However, they should have had plenty of exposure to spoken English to hear the words in context first, and will also benefit from matching the words to picture cards (NALDIC, 2011).

Taking it further

For more information and signposting about synthetic phonics and learning EAL go to the website of the National Association of Language Development in the Curriculum (www.naldic.org.uk/eal-teaching-and-learning/faqs/EAL-synthetic-phonics).

When young children are learning to read, as well as using phonic knowledge they need to be able to draw on other strategies such as using grammatical knowledge, and the overall context of the sentence. This is particularly difficult for EAL learners because they will generally understand fewer words than the other children in the group. This underlines the importance of teaching language comprehension alongside synthetic phonics. EAL learners will benefit from the following:

- The use of pictures and objects during synthetic phonics sessions. For example, showing children pictures when segmenting words such as 'tub', 'log', 'hat', 'bin' and 'sock'.
- Putting words into sentences to put them into context and give them meaning. For example, 'S-a-t, sat. I sat on a chair.'
- During shared reading, pointing to pictures after decoding particular words.
- Pausing to look at the pictures and talk about what is happening.
- Choosing books for guided, shared and independent reading that feature scenarios and topics that the children have some knowledge of and will be able to identify with.
- Giving children plenty of time to talk together throughout the day in order to develop English-language comprehension.

All together now

"All children love stories like 'Bear Hunt', and you can see how pleased our EAL learners are that they are able to join in with the others."

Repetition is key to helping children learning EAL pick up and retain new language and vocabulary.

Children who are learning EAL will especially benefit from regularly revisiting books, rhymes and songs with repeated refrains. Not only do story and rhyme put language into context, but the repetition of key vocabulary and phrases helps children commit language to memory and encourages them to join in and recite it. Try the following:

- **Nursery rhymes:** Ten in the Bed, There was an Old Lady Who Swallowed a Fly, The Wheels on the Bus, Five Currant Buns, This Little Piggy and Polly Put the Kettle On.
- **Fairy tales:** Three Little Pigs, Three Billy Goats Gruff, Goldilocks and the Three Bears, The Enormous Turnip, The Gingerbread Man and Chicken Licken.
- **Picture books:** *We're Going on a Bear Hunt* by Michael Rosen (Walker), *Farmer Duck* by Martin Waddell (Walker), *Handa's Surprise* by Eileen Browne (Walker), *The Smartest Giant in Town* by Julia Donaldson (Macmillan), *Brown Bear, Brown Bear, What Do You See?* by Bill Martin Jr. (Puffin), *We're Going on a Picnic* by Pat Hutchins (Red Fox) and *Have You Seen My Cat?* by Eric Carle (Puffin).

Teaching tip

Use visual aids such as large sequencing cards so the children can see what is coming next. Yellow Door (www.yellow-door.net) has produced resource packs that include story sequencing cards for a range of well known children's stories.

Taking it further

Choose a story and a rhyme of the week and repeat them each day. Play audio versions on the listening centre and provide puppets, sequencing cards and props for the children to retell and recite them independently.

Dual-language books

"We have dual-language picture books here, but I'm not really sure how to use them."

There are many benefits to using dual-language storybooks, both for children who are learning EAL and their English-speaking peers.

Sharing dual-language picture books not only encourages EAL learners to use and read English, but it helps to make all children aware of the appearance of different language scripts. What's more, it helps English-speaking children develop an appreciation of the challenge faced by EAL learners as they learn to read and write in a foreign language. Following are some tips for using a dual-language picture book.

- Begin by introducing the story and explaining that it is written in two languages. Point out and name the English script and the other language.
- Explain that you will read the whole book in English first, then again in the other language (unless you choose to read the translations page by page).
- Read the book as you would any other, pausing to look at the pictures and asking the children questions about the story as you go along.
- Pick out key words and repeat them both in English and the other language.
- If you are unable to read the script of the alternative language, ask a support assistant to read the translation or source audio versions of the book in different languages.

Story bags

"Oh wow, look I what found in here!"

Use stories to give children who are new to English some background context on which to build further learning.

Practitioners teaching children who are new to English are advised to frame the curriculum around the children's knowledge and experiences. In the early years many children have limited experiences, and so it can help to plan topics against the background context of a story. Put together a bag of props, puppets, games and activity ideas that can be used to re-enact a story, explore links and themes, and extend topical language and vocabulary. A story bag might contain:

- Dual-language versions of the featured story. If you cannot find one, ask support assistants or parents to provide a written translation of the text.
- A selection of objects and artefacts that are featured in the story, together with vocabulary cards that name each object in a variety of languages.
- Puppets and story sequencing cards for retelling the story.
- Laminated photos of places, animals and people that will encourage observational comments.
- Information books with large, good-quality pictures and photos for developing language related to the themes of the story.
- Jigsaw puzzles and games linked to story themes that will help children extend their vocabulary.
- An audio version of the story in a variety of different languages.

Teaching tip

Before reading a story in English introduce key vocabulary with the help of real objects and artefacts, and give children the word both in English and their first language. Also, introduce the characters by pointing to their pictures and saying their names.

Taking it further

Find inspiration for creating your own story bags in *The Little Book of Story Bags* by Marianne Sargent (Featherstone Education). Also, Storysack has produced a selection for EAL learners (www.storysack.com).

Bonus idea ★

Make story boxes using decorated shoe boxes that serve as dioramas and contain finger puppets and props, or story boards with background scenes and stick-on characters. Use these to retell stories and for sequencing activities.

Treasure hunting

"I find it!"

As well as being great fun, treasure hunts make children aware of the purpose of print, give them a reason to read, get them talking together and encourage cooperation.

EAL learners can gain a great deal from participating in a treasure hunt. They learn about the directionality of the English language as they attempt to read or watch others read the clues; they are encouraged to talk with their peers about what the clue means and where they should go next; and they are included in an enjoyable group activity.

- Use treasure hunts to introduce positional language and directional language.
- Design clues so that they teach vocabulary associated with shape, colour or objects. For example 'Find the square', 'Look behind the blue curtains' or 'Look under the big table'.
- Group EAL learners with children who have good reading skills and are able to decode written instructions and clues such as 'Go to the shed' or 'Look next to the tree'.
- Add translations to the clues in the children's first languages for more able children or bilingual support assistants to read out.

Taking it further

Read *The Treasure Hunt* by Nick Butterworth (HarperCollins) and challenge the children to make up their own treasure hunts with picture clues. This will foster English language development in EAL learners as they look at and talk about the pictures with their peers.

Bonus idea ★

Set up a role-play pirate ship and leave some treasure maps on board leading to treasure chests hidden around the outdoor area. All the children will be excited by this, and those who are new to English will be exposed to language associated with pirates, treasure, ships, the ocean, map reading, direction and position.

Multilingual book corner

"It's so lovely. She comes in every Wednesday and spends the whole afternoon reading to the children in both English and Urdu. Her little girl is so pleased to see her, and the other children are fascinated by the sound of Urdu spoken so fluently."

Adapt your book corner so that it is just as welcoming and relevant to children who speak EAL.

Set up your book corner so that it is comfortable and inviting. Provide cushioned chairs, giant beanbags and an alphabet mat or rug. Ensure that the area is well lit so that the children can see the books clearly.

- Display illustrated poems and rhymes in different languages.
- Set up a story board and change it to focus on a different story each week. Display pictures of the characters and objects from the story. For example, you might show three pigs, some straw, sticks and bricks, three houses built of each material and a wolf. Stick on labels in English and other relevant languages.
- Place multicultural persona dolls and character puppets in the corner for the children to read to.
- Set up a listening centre and provide a selection of multilingual story CDs for the children to listen to.
- Stock the shelves with dual-language picture books.
- Provide story jigsaws for the children to put together and talk about.

Taking it further

Involve the children in drawing and painting pictures to add to the story board.

Involving parents

Invite parents to come into the setting and spend some time sharing books with the children in the book corner. Explain the importance of first language development and how helpful it would be to have them come in and read to the children in their home languages.

Bonus idea ★

Look on the Internet for multilingual books that you can read online for free. The International Children's Digital Library has a large selection, which you will find at http://en.childrenslibrary.org.

Library visit

"We take a small group to visit the library every Friday. It's great because they've got a much better selection of dual-language books that we do."

Local libraries welcome visits from early years settings and schools, and many have a good selection of books and resources for EAL learners.

Invite parents to come on the library visit. Take the opportunity to introduce those parents who have not yet used the facility to the resources that are available to them. Remember, libraries are a good source of local knowledge and can signpost parents to useful support services.

Take the children on a visit to your local library. Ensure that your EAL learners get the most out of the visit by phoning and asking the library staff if they would be able to pull out a selection of multicultural and dual-language books ahead of your arrival. They may even have some bilingual staff who would be willing to read a story to the children. Use your visit to:

- **Talk about travel arrangements:** Discuss possible options such as walking, driving by car or catching a bus. Use picture cards to help EAL learners understand the reasoning – for instance cards showing lots of children, a car and a bus to decide which they would fit into and a map of the route with cards showing a bus and footprint to decide whether it would be quicker by bus or on foot.
- **Talk about books:** Take the children around the library in small groups and look at the different books on offer. Introduce vocabulary to describe 'storybooks', 'information books', 'magazines', 'audiobooks' and 'computers'.
- **Borrow some books:** Allow the children to choose some books to borrow and take back to the setting. Follow up the visit with regular future visits to return and exchange the books.

Different scripts

"Of course it makes sense that her mark making would be so full of curls, loops and squiggles, because that's what she sees at home."

Like all young children, EAL learners will need to develop an understanding of the basic concepts about print both in English and their home language before they will be able to read and write.

EAL learners' attempts at writing will be heavily influenced by the print they see in their home and learning environment. As a result their early mark making may resemble a mixture of scripts and include letters and symbols from both languages (Soni, 2013). Help these children to discriminate between different language scripts by taking the following into consideration:

- Although many languages use the same alphabet as English, some will have fewer or more letters and characters, while others will use an entirely different script. Help children identify print and understand that it carries meaning by displaying words, labels and signs all over the learning environment in a variety of different languages.
- English script is written from left to right and from top to bottom but some children may have observed their parents reading and writing in a different direction. Read dual-language storybooks and point out the two different scripts. Talk about the difference between the appearance of each script and which direction each script is read in.
- Before children can write they need plenty of practise with forming the key handwriting movements. Involve the children in physical games and exercises that practise large movements associated with English handwriting directionality, but that also demonstrate the movements associated with other language scripts, and get the children to compare and contrast.

Teaching tip

Write EAL learners' names in English script as well as the script of their home language on coat pegs, drawers, self-registration cards and snack cards.

A reason to write

"She draws the most elaborate maps and they are covered in labels. I can't read them but she knows what they mean."

Foster emergent writing by providing a variety of resources and activities that will inspire all the children in your setting.

As is the case with reading, children are encouraged to write if they are surrounded by a print-rich environment. They will also be encouraged by the provision of a range of mark-making tools and resources, both indoors and outside. Try the following:

- Fill large shallow trays such as Tuff Spots (see Idea 52) with damp sand, and provide sticks for the children to draw patterns and write with.
- Provide clipboards, paper and pens so that the children can move around while they draw pictures and write notes.
- Set up easels next to activities so children can 'sign up' to have a go.
- Put out handheld whiteboards and pens, and playground chalks in the outdoor area.
- Think about how you can incorporate writing into role-play: leave notepads, pencils and pens next to telephones; hang calendars and provide diaries for use in the travel agent; give police notepads to take notes; provide a receipt book in the shop; and give waiting staff small order pads.
- Set up easels next to games equipment to encourage the children to record their scores.
- Hide treasure maps for the children to discover, and provide them with tea-stained paper to create their own.
- Leave architects' plans in the construction area and provide large sheets of paper with pencils and rulers for the children to draw their own.

Learning EAL outdoors

Part 9

Let's go outside

"He is much more talkative when he's outdoors."

The outdoor environment is particularly conducive to language learning.

There are a number of reasons why the outdoor environment fosters the development of communication and language skills in young children.

- **Freedom:** When outside, children have more freedom to move around and make a noise, which encourages imaginative and creative play. Children who are enthusiastic about their play are more eager to communicate with each other and will make a greater effort to get others to understand them as they strive to express their opinions and share their ideas.
- **Space:** Some children may feel less inhibited about communicating in their first language or attempting to speak English when they are outside in an open space.
- **Peace and quiet:** Unlike indoors, noise floats away in the open air, making it easier for children to hear each other as they play and talk outside. This reduces the effort required from those children who are already struggling to put their thoughts into English. If they are constantly required to repeat and make themselves heard they might eventually give up. Being able to hear each other also has implications for learning English because children need to be able to hear others talking if they are to absorb the language.
- **Hands-on active experiences:** When outdoors children can get involved in role-play, large-scale construction, physical activity and messy play. All of these experiences help children develop an understanding of basic concepts, and the accompanying social interaction and discussion that takes place introduces them to a wide range of vocabulary and phrases.

Surprise in the ice

"It's freezer!"

This hands-on activity appeals to the senses and is particularly helpful for building vocabulary and developing language.

In the early years children need to physically investigate everything around them. It is through hands-on exploration that children learn about the world and develop the language they need to make sense of it. This is particularly true for children learning EAL. The following activity excites children and encourages them to talk together about what they can see and feel, making it a great conversation starter and vocabulary builder.

- Begin by choosing some everyday objects and toys that the children will easily recognise.
- Place these objects inside variously sized and shaped containers, for example ice-cream tubs, buckets and jelly moulds.
- Fill each container with water.
- Add food colouring, glitter, glass pebbles and shredded tissue paper to the different containers to help hide or disguise the object inside.
- Freeze the containers overnight.
- The following day place the ice blocks in the water tray outside and invite the children to come and investigate. Encourage them to talk about how the ice feels when they touch it. Allow children who speak EAL to use words in their first language and offer the English translation. Introduce language to describe the colours and textures.
- As the ice melts encourage the children to describe what is happening. Introduce vocabulary associated with freezing and melting. Can the children identify and name the object that is being gradually revealed?

Teaching tip

Take a camera and clipboard outside and jot down any comments the children make. These valuable observations can be used as evidence of learning in the children's profiles.

Taking it further

Invite children who speak EAL to help make some mystery ice cubes for others to investigate. Ask them to choose and name an object to freeze and use the opportunity to describe the shapes of the containers and introduce key words about the freezing process.

Changing seasons

"There is just so much to see and talk about when we are outside."

Use seasonal changes as a springboard for learning language related to a wide range of subjects.

All young children, including those who are learning EAL, pick up language by hearing it used within meaningful contexts. Take the children outside to witness the changing of the seasons first-hand, and use this experience to introduce new language and vocabulary.

- **Clothing:** Help the children decide what is the most appropriate clothing to wear in different weather. Talk about how the weather makes them feel: 'cold', 'warm', 'hot', 'sweaty' or 'wet'. Help them choose what they should wear: 'waterproof coat', 'sunhat', 'trousers', 'shorts', 'jumper', 'Wellington boots' or 'sandals'. Describe the clothing they are putting on: 'thick red jumper', 'light blue T-shirt' or 'green crocodile wellies'.
- **Senses:** Go outside in all weathers and talk about the different sensations the children experience. For instance, the feel of the 'breeze in their hair', 'warmth of sun on their skin', 'slop and slurp of muddy puddles', 'spray of rain on their faces' and 'crunch of snow under foot'.
- **Sounds:** Get the children to listen to everything around them. What can they hear? 'Cars', 'trains', 'aeroplanes', 'birds', 'the wind', 'music', 'dogs' or 'the sea'.
- **Changes:** Talk about what the weather is like in the 'spring', 'summer', 'autumn' and 'winter'. Is it 'cold', 'warm', 'dry' or 'wet' Look at the 'plants', 'trees' and 'flowers'. How do they change at different times of year? Describe the colours, and collect and make collages out of 'petals', 'leaves', 'blossoms', 'buds', 'fruits' and 'seeds'.

Sand play

"He would happily spend all day playing in the sand if he could."

The sand tray is a great resource for language development and vocabulary building.

The sand tray not only enables children to explore the properties of sand, but serves as a backdrop for imaginative and small world play. Join children as they play in the sand, and introduce nouns and verbs that describe what they are using and doing. Furthermore, link sand play to current themes with the addition of toys and objects that will help the children learn a range of topical vocabulary.

- Use sand play to introduce language that describes the texture, appearance and physical state of dry, wet and damp sand.
- Provide sieves, spades, buckets, sand moulds and rakes, and talk about how the sand feels and what happens when you try to build with it, shape it and draw in it.
- Bury a treasure chest filled with precious objects such as glass pebbles, plastic jewels, metal coins and costume jewellery. When the children discover it, examine the treasure and introduce vocabulary that describes colours, textures and materials.
- Add shells to the sand and use them to teach vocabulary that describes shape, colour and pattern.
- Set up a small world beach scene and use it to teach the children language associated with the seaside and beach holidays.
- Set up a small world pirate scene and use it to teach the children language associated with pirate ships, islands and buried treasure.
- Bury everyday objects and as the children dig each item up introduce vocabulary to name the object, talk about what it does and describe its shape and colour.

Teaching tip

Try not to overwhelm children with a bombardment of words and phrases. Introduce a little at a time and use plenty of repetition to help them absorb the new language.

Bonus idea ★

Sand is not the only thing you can fill a sand tray with. Try beads, dried coloured rice and pasta, beans and pulses, flax seeds, leaves, conkers or soft bark.

Water play

"It splashed . . . there was too much water in!"

Water is an extremely versatile resource that can be used to develop language and vocabulary in a variety of ways.

The following ideas demonstrate how water can be used to teach EAL learners vocabulary and phrases related to a range of concepts and themes.

- Use water play to introduce language that describes the texture, appearance and physical states of water and ice.
- Provide jugs, beakers, funnels, sieves, water wheels, watering cans and sponges, and talk about how the water feels and behaves when you pour it, sprinkle it and squeeze it out. Fill and empty a range of containers and talk about and compare the different sizes in relation to the volumes of water they can hold.
- Fill water balloons from an outside tap. Increase and decrease the pressure and introduce vocabulary that describes what happens. Throw the balloons and talk about what happens as they hit the walls and floor.
- Give the children pieces of guttering, crates, hurdle stands and buckets and help them to build a waterway. As you work together talk about how you are positioning the equipment. Use jugs and watering cans to pour water on to the waterway. Describe how the water moves and the direction it travels. Add small boats and try to get them moving as well.
- Turn the water tray into a rockpool. Add rocks, pebbles, sand, shells and toy sea creatures, and use the scene to introduce names and descriptions.
- Float toy boats in different shapes, colours and sizes. Describe and compare the boats, load them up with stones and pebbles and talk about floating and sinking.

Sight-seeing

"I seed the high tower."

Go out for a walk to introduce vocabulary associated with shape, space and measure.

When teaching children who are new to English about the basic concepts that underpin shape, space and measure it is helpful to give them concrete examples and visual clues. Take the children out on a walk to look at and talk about the features of the natural and built environment while putting the associated vocabulary into context.

- **Shape:** Look at the shapes of buildings, roofs, signs, vehicles and natural objects. Name the shapes and describe their characteristics.
- **Space:** Talk about where you are going as you walk. Explain which direction you are travelling in, how far it is to get to a certain point and where different places are in relation to you. Point out when you walk over, under, through or around something.
- **Measure:** Look at and compare the size of different objects. Pick up natural items to find out how much they weigh. Point out different-sized vehicles and talk about how big the load is that they are carrying or how many people might fit in the back.

Teaching tip

Take the children in small groups so everyone has a chance to speak. Mix children who are learning EAL with English speakers so they can hear their peers giving descriptions in English. Allow the children to use whichever language they choose.

Bonus idea ★

Teach children about pattern by showing them samples of carpets, wallpapers and fabrics from different cultures, and pictures of architecture from countries around the world. Talk about and describe the shapes and designs.

Minibeast hotel

"We have only got a small tarmacked outdoor area, so we built a minibeast hotel and were surprised at what moved in."

Minibeasts are fascinating to young children and very useful for language development because they come in so many different colours and shapes, and with so many varied features.

Build your own minibeast hotel in your outdoor area to attract as many of these small creatures as you can, so the children can observe them first-hand.

- Choose a quiet, damp place in the outdoor area where minibeasts are likely to be.
- Lay several flat wooden pallets on top of each other to create a tower, nailing each to the one below so that they stand securely without risk of topping over.
- Line some pallets with offcuts of old carpet and push dry leaves, pieces of broken roof slate, pipes, bamboo sticks, stones and chunks of grass turf into the gaps so there are plenty of nooks and crannies for little creatures to hide inside.
- Provide bug collectors and magnifiers for the children to look for, observe and study the creatures that move in. Provide information books with good clear pictures for the children to look up what they find. Introduce the English names of the minibeasts and ask the children what they are called in other languages.
- Spend time with the children observing the minibeasts and encourage them to describe what they find and see in whichever language they choose, while you offer the English terms and vocabulary.
- Ask children from other countries if they have different minibeasts where they come from. Search on the Internet for photos that they can use to show you what they mean.

Taking it further

Plant flowers with bright colours and strong scents to attract bees and butterflies to your garden area.

Bonus idea ★

Create a temporary pond using a large, deep, water tray. Dig out a patch in your garden area and drop the tray in. Line the bottom of the tray with a scattering of soil or sand and add some pond plants and rocks. Watch and wait to see what moves in.

Move it

"We go outside and play a couple of games together at least once a day."

When children play physical games they learn vocabulary associated with the body, movement, direction and sport.

Playing games like this is helpful to children learning EAL because rather than being under pressure to offer a verbal response, they are required to listen to an instruction and follow it. If they do not understand they can look around them and imitate what the other children are doing. Try the following simple suggestions:

- **Traffic lights:** Tell the children they should walk on orange, run on green and stop on red. Hold up table tennis bats covered in green, orange and red paper and call out the words 'walk', 'run' and 'stop'.
- **Follow the leader:** Choose a child to lead everyone in a line, calling out instructions such as 'march', 'skip', 'stop' and 'turn around'.
- **Heads, shoulders, knees and toes:** Sing the song and name the body parts.
- **Move like me:** Stand in a circle and instruct the children to do actions such as 'five star jumps', 'three hops', 'four turns on the spot' or 'crouch down low'.
- **Stand up if . . . :** Get the children to spread out and sit down in a space. Call out instructions such as 'stand up if you have brown hair', 'stand up if you are wearing a jumper', 'sit down if you have long hair' or 'sit down if your shoes have laces'.
- **Ball games:** Play ball games such as football, tennis, basketball and catch. Introduce vocabulary such as 'bounce', 'roll', 'kick', 'throw', 'catch' and 'aim'.

All about bubbles

"It in the sky. Look! I got it!"

Children really enjoy playing with bubbles, and they are surprisingly versatile in terms of language learning.

The following activities use bubbles in a variety of ways to introduce language and vocabulary associated with a range of themes.

- **Bursting bubbles:** Take some bubble liquid and a bubble blower outside to a large space. Blow the bubbles and challenge the children to burst as many as they can before they touch the floor. Point out how high the bubbles go, count how many the children manage to burst and talk about how they float and blow about on the breeze.
- **Giant bubbles:** Fill a paddling pool with bubble liquid and drop in a hula hoop. Get the children to take turns to stand in the pool and lift the hoop out of the water to create a giant bubble. Marvel at how big, large and enormous the bubbles are and that the children can stand inside them.
- **Bubble prints:** Mix some bubble liquid and paint in some large trays. Give the children straws and ask them to blow into the liquid to make bubbles. Delicately lay pieces of paper on the bubbles and lift them to reveal bubble prints. Name the different colours, talk about how the bubbles are created, and describe the circular shapes on the prints. Remind the children to blow through the straws and not to suck the liquid up.

Teddy bears' picnic

"The children love going on picnics, and they give us so much to talk about."

A teddy bears' picnic is a fun way of putting language and vocabulary into a purposeful context.

Young children, and especially children who are learning EAL, learn by seeing and doing. Each stage in the process of a teddy bears' picnic offers opportunities to introduce a wide range of vocabulary.

- **Invite some bears:** Send home invitations to the children's bears, asking them to come in on a certain day for a picnic.
- **Choose a venue:** Show the children photos of possible local picnic venues and discuss why some are better than others. Ask the children what they can see in the photos, point to things and use facial expressions to illustrate why they are good or bad points.
- **Buy the food:** Look at some pictures of picnic foods, name them in different languages and write a shopping list together. Ask the children for their ideas about what is usually eaten on a picnic. Go out to the local shop to select and buy the food. Take the opportunity to introduce vocabulary related to food, shopping and money.
- **Prepare the food:** Involve the children in making sandwiches and cakes. Talk about likes and dislikes, again using facial expressions and gestures to show how you feel about different foods. Introduce vocabulary linked to cooking and kitchen utensils.
- **Go on the picnic:** Go on the picnic together, and describe and compare everyone's bears. Take the opportunity to talk about and repeat the language introduced during the planning and preparations.

Taking it further

Link the experience to stories such as *We're Going on a Picnic* by Pat Hutchins (Red Fox), *Picnic* by John Burningham (Red Fox) and *The Teddy Bears' Picnic* by Jerry Garcia and David Grisman (HarperFestival).

Involving parents

Invite parents to come along on the picnic with the children and their bears.

Nature collages

"This is my best shell. It is white with pink bits."

Use natural objects to create pictures and collages and help children build a bank of vocabulary about nature, colour and pattern.

Taking it further

Take photos of the collages and use them to make photo books. Look at these books later to talk about how each picture was created, and revise the associated vocabulary.

Bonus idea ★

Give the children small plastic mirrors so they can see themselves. Organise them into pairs and challenge them to use natural objects to make pictures of each other. Use the activity to name facial features and talk about hair, eye and skin colour. Take photos of the pictures and use them to make a book of faces, with a collage, photo and child's name on each page.

Go outside to collect a range of natural objects, and use them to create temporary pictures and collages on the floor. Craft activities like this provide the context EAL learners need to process and remember new language and vocabulary.

- **At the park:** Collect items such as conkers, leaves, sycamore seeds, acorns and reeds to create pictures of animals. Take laminated pictures of animals outside with you and show them to the children. Help the children select objects according to colour and texture, for example chestnut cases for spiky hedgehogs, and hare's tall grass for rabbits.
- **In the garden:** Challenge the children to use the petals and seeds from sunflowers, daisy and dandelion heads, leaves, stones, sand and long grass to make pictures of anything they like.
- **At the beach:** Collect shells, seaweed, pebbles, shingle and driftwood to create collages of fish and sea animals. Encourage the children to closely examine the different colours, shapes and patterns on the shells as they work.

Observation, assessment and planning

Part 10

Right to access the curriculum

"Really, when you think about it, children learning EAL learn in the same way as any other child. It's all about giving them first-hand experiences that they can use to find meaning."

Part of a foundation stage practitioner's task is to ensure that all children are able to access the early years curriculum. Children who are learning EAL can be afforded the same opportunities as all other children if practitioners plan active learning experiences that put language into context.

Involving parents

Send home a translated planning web each time you begin a new topic to keep parents informed and involved. Ask parents with specialist knowledge or skills to come in and help with particular topics.

The Statutory Framework for the EYFS (DfE, 2014) identifies three characteristics of effective learning for all young children: playing and exploring, active learning and creating and thinking critically. However, these are just as applicable to EAL learners, if not more so.

Playing and exploring

- Children are much more likely to remember the meanings of words if they can link them to concrete experiences. You can help children add to their banks of vocabulary by playing alongside them while offering a rich verbal commentary, for example 'I used the big red bucket to make my sandcastle, and – look – you chose the small blue one.'
- You can also ensure that children who are unfamiliar with English are more fully engaged by building on their interests and starting with what they know. In the beginning study topics that they can easily relate to such as 'ourselves' or 'favourite toys'.

Active learning

- If children are given time and space to become more deeply involved in their play and investigations they will show higher levels of concentration and be more motivated to persist with an activity. EAL learners will be more inclined to attempt speaking English if they are involved and interested in what they are doing. This means you need to observe the children to find out what they are interested in and plan learning experiences that build on these interests.

- Ensure that children learning EAL are fully involved by using visual aids when introducing unfamiliar topics and themes and learning useful key words in the children's first languages.

Creating and thinking critically

- EAL learners are just as capable as their English-speaking peers and have the same potential to become creative and critical thinkers. Have high expectations and bear in mind that although they may not be able to verbalise their thoughts in English, they may very well be thinking of some complex ideas in their first language.
- Resist the temptation to dumb down your conversation with children learning EAL. Instead respond to them by providing the English language they need using simple descriptions with plenty of repetition.
- Allow all children to make their own choices about how to do things. EAL learners may not be able to tell you what they are thinking but they will be able to show you their knowledge and ideas through the things that they do.

Involving parents

Towards the end of each day, print off a photographic timeline of the day to hand out to parents. Add a caption to each picture with translated versions for parents of children who are learning EAL. Ask parents to look at these with their children and discuss the day in their home language to help consolidate their learning by making links between English and their home language. (Remember to get parental permission with regard to distributing photos of children before you do this.)

Early days

"She doesn't say anything, and even if she did I wouldn't be able to understand her to know if she's making any sense."

The first task you will have when a non-English-speaking child starts at your setting will be to assess their language skills. Of course their speaking and understanding may be very good in their first language; however, this will be difficult for you to assess if you cannot speak their language as well.

Teaching tip

Meet regularly with the other practitioners in the setting to talk about EAL learners' progress, discuss strategies that are working and think about next steps.

When assessing a non-English-speaking child's first-language skills:

- Speak to their parents. Ask them for their opinion about their child's language development. If the parents cannot speak English ask an interpreter to help.
- Ask a bilingual support assistant to spend some time with the child and assess their language skills.
- Ask the local authority if they can provide some temporary support.
- Write to any early years settings that they attended in their home country and ask for copies of assessments and reports.
- Ask parents if they can bring in their child's learning journeys or equivalent from the previous setting.

When assessing a child's acquisition of the English language:

- Look for recognition in their facial expressions when you speak to them.
- Look for smiles or frowns when they are playing that demonstrate their understanding of other children's comments.
- Look for puzzled or vacant expressions that demonstrate a lack of understanding.
- Watch to see if they are following simple instructions and daily routines without copying or following others.

Taking it further

Listen out for EAL learners beginning to mix English words in with their first language. This is a sign that they are beginning to internalise the English language.

Assessing progress

"It would really help if I had some idea of the different stages involved in acquiring a new language."

Hester (1990) identifies four stages in English language learning to help educators identify where EAL learners are in their English-language development.

Hester points out that because children develop in different ways not all will follow the same sequence.

Stage 1: New to English
- Joins in but may not speak, and uses gestures.
- Watches others and imitates/echoes words and phrases.
- Uses first language in most contexts but knows some English words.
- Begins to put English words together to make simple phrases.

Stage 2: Becoming familiar with English
- Understands more English and moves between first language and English.
- Has a growing vocabulary for naming objects; begins to describe and expand phrases.
- Becomes more accurate, for example, with pronouns and tenses.

Stage 3: Becoming confident as a user of English
- Shows growing command of English grammar and makes more complex sentences.
- Pronounces English words in an increasingly similar way to native English speakers.
- Has an increasing vocabulary related to a broader range of subjects.

Stage 4: Very fluent user of English in most social and learning contexts
- Exceptionally fluent in many contexts.
- Needs support with language play.
- Confident in conversation.
- Moves with ease between English and first language, depending on context.

Teaching tip

In the early years the most accurate assessment of a child's language development will come from observation. Observe the children in a variety of contexts such as play, group time, story time and focused activities, and look at how they communicate with different children and members of staff, outside professionals and parents. This should give you a more rounded view of their language development.

Online resource: assessment sheet

Emotional needs

"We thought he was getting along fine, but then I did a focused observation on him and realised he was tending to play alongside the others rather than with them."

Children who are happy and confident will be more successful learners. Children who have a negative self-image and low self-esteem will be unable to focus and concentrate, and this will impact on their learning.

Children who are learning EAL may be quiet when they first join an early years setting due to a combination of factors. They will most likely be observing the customs and behaviours of those around them and listening to the new language. However, they may also be feeling isolated and unhappy, worrying about where their place is in this new environment and how they can possibly communicate with the other children.

It is imperative that you take time to assess newcomers' social and emotional needs during their first couple of months in the setting. Observe these children and consider how they are playing and interacting. Ask yourself:

- Do they appear to be settling in?
- Do they seem to be building in confidence?
- What do they enjoy doing the most? Is there anything that appears to upset, annoy or frustrate them?
- Are they participating or simply observing?
- Are they forming any relationships with the other children?
- What are their social skills like? Are they sharing and cooperating with others?
- Are they showing any signs of frustration or anger when communicating with others?

Get organised

"There just aren't enough hours in the day."

Observation, assessment and record keeping are time consuming. However, this is a vital part of effective early years practice, and so it is essential to ensure that everyone has the time and resources to carry out observations and maintain good records.

Observation is usually the first thing to be pushed by the wayside in a busy early years setting. This is particularly true in reception classes, where teachers are under so much pressure to produce results in literacy and mathematics. Try the following strategies to ensure that observation is fully integrated into everyday practice.

- Plan to give every member of staff allocated observation time. Explain to the children that staff are unavailable when they are doing observations, and should not be interrupted unless it is very important. Wearing a tiara, crown or hat is a good way of signalling that you are carrying out an observation.
- Provide practitioners with clipboards holding group lists and printed observation pro formas, as well as bum bags containing pens, sticky notes, cameras and MP3 recorders.
- Keep a checklist to monitor which children have been observed, and when. Highlight those children who will benefit from additional observation, including children learning EAL.
- Give all staff members time once a week to transfer snapshot observations into learning journeys, print off photo observations and write accompanying notes, collate work samples and file focused observations.
- Give key workers with new children who speak EAL extra time to fit more observations in so they can closely monitor their progress.

Taking it further

Timetable regular whole-staff meetings to discuss observations and ensure that they are used to inform ongoing planning.

Bonus idea ★

Allocate space on planning documents for assessment notes, and refer to these when thinking about next steps.

Well supported

"I don't know where I'd be without her."

Experienced and well-qualified support assistants are worth their weight in gold. Use them effectively to ensure that you provide the best possible support for the EAL learners in your setting.

> **Bonus idea** ★
>
> Contact your local authority and find out if there are any advanced skills practitioners in your area who specialise in EAL. They may be able to visit your setting and share their expertise with you and your support assistants.

When you first take on a teaching or lead professional role the job can seem overwhelming. With the large amount of paperwork and daily preparation involved you will need all the help you can get, and your support assistants will prove invaluable. However, it is important to think carefully about how you organise their time and use their skills in order to get the best from them.

- Find out if there are any local training courses about EAL that your support assistants can attend. Ask your local authority if it will fund such training and, if not, who else might.
- Listen to any ideas or suggestions that support assistants offer. They might have a great deal more experience when it comes to working with children learning EAL, and you may benefit from a new perspective.
- Make the best use of your assistants' unique sets of skills. Think about where their strengths lie and organise your planning with this in mind.
- If you need your assistants to help out with tasks like photocopying or laminating, try to ensure they do this before and after the children arrive in the setting or during activities when the children need less support, such as PE or music and movement.

Collecting snapshots

"Sandeep responded to the instruction 'go and wash your hands before lunch'."

As an early years practitioner you will find yourself constantly making mental notes when you notice a child do or say something significant. Snapshot observations are especially helpful for assessing the progress of EAL learners, because much of this assessment is based on noticing subtle progress such as when they use a particular word or phrase in English for the first time.

There are several different ways that you can manage snapshot observations.

- Practitioners from smaller settings may prefer to carry a notebook and pen with them to jot down anything interesting the children say or do. The drawback to this method is that these notes need to be transferred to the children's learning journeys.
- Many settings use sticky notes and stick them temporarily on to a 'Look what we've been learning' wall display featuring all the children's names or photos. Such a display is helpful because it gives practitioners an idea of how many snapshot observations they have taken of each child at a glance. However, the information on the sticky notes either has to be transferred to the children's learning journeys or the sticky notes have to be glued in.
- A further option is to create a template for a sheet of stickers, attach ready-printed sheets to a clipboard and fill them in each time you notice something. On each sticker list the following headings: 'Date', 'Child's name', 'Observer's name', 'Area of learning' and 'Observation'. These are great time savers because they simply need peeling and sticking into learning journeys.

Teaching tip

Create a spreadsheet that lists the children's names down one side and the areas of learning across the top. Each time you transfer your snapshot observations to the children's learning journeys, tick them off on the spreadsheet. This will give you a good overview of how many observations you have collected in each area of learning, and will highlight if any children have been slipping under the radar.

Online resource: template for sheet of snapshot observation stickers

Focused observations

"We know when she's watching and listening, because she wears the crown."

Observation tells practitioners a great deal about how a child is developing across all areas of learning. It is particularly helpful to carry out regular observations on new children during their first few months to monitor how they are settling in and whether they are making progress.

Crosse (2007) explains that focused observations are particularly helpful for monitoring the progress of children who are learning EAL because:

- Observation is less stressful than testing. Children who feel uncomfortable or under pressure are unlikely to perform well in a language test, and practitioners will be able to glean much more about their language development through observing them in play situations.
- Observation gives practitioners a more rounded view of how a child is developing and progressing. In the case of EAL learners observation is useful for finding out how settled and happy a child is, how well they are accessing the environment, who they are interacting with, how well they are following routines and responding to instructions, which language they are using most frequently and if they are employing any helpful or unhelpful coping strategies.

Note down the following:

- The context of the observation – for instance, whether the child is playing alone, in a pair or in a group, whether they are playing indoors or outside, whether they are engaged in a familiar activity or attempting something for the first time and whether the activity is self or adult-initiated. Each of these factors will have an impact on the child's learning.

- Which language the child is using, and whether they are switching between languages. Also, which languages the respondent is using. This is important because children may respond differently and demonstrate varying levels of knowledge and understanding in different languages.

Taking it further

Tracking observations will enable you to find out how well a child is accessing the learning environment. Print off a plan of the setting and observe for five minutes every half an hour or so throughout the session. Using a different-coloured pen each time, mark on the plan how long the child stays in each area and draw lines to show where they move to. This will show you if they are staying in a particular area, flitting around or settling at each activity for a reasonable amount of time.

Captured on film

"We use video all the time. It's great as an observation method because it captures everything; what the children are doing, what they say, how they behave, and their facial expressions too."

Video and audio recordings are an effective way of monitoring children's language development over time. If done regularly they can help to create a comprehensive overview of EAL learners' progress.

Create an ongoing record of children's language development over time by taking regular recordings of their verbal interactions.

- Record the children in a variety of different contexts, for example when engaged in role-play, playing on their own and using self-speech, and during adult-led focused activities. This will give you a more rounded picture of their language development.
- Store the recordings on a password-protected computer. Create a file for each child and label each recording with the date it was taken.
- The visual content in video recordings will provide some context; however, this will be missing in the audio recordings. It is therefore helpful to create an accompanying document with details of what the activity was, where it took place, when, and who else was present.

Planning for EAL learners

"I've found that what works for EAL learners also works for the other children."

The underlying principles of planning for children learning EAL are much the same as for all children in the early years. Practitioners should plan to provide active, hands-on activities and purposeful tasks that enable children to link language and basic concepts to concrete experiences.

There are many specific activity ideas as well as guidance on how to plan the learning environment within this book. However, below is some general guidance for planning to include children learning EAL:

- Plan activities that build on the children's interests so that they are motivated to learn.
- Plan activities that start with what the children know so that they have a familiar reference to relate back to.
- Plan plenty of small group activities as opposed to whole-class teaching so that all children get a chance to participate.
- Organise groups so that children who speak the same language are together and are encouraged to use their first language.
- Use play as the main vehicle for learning, because it places language within a meaningful context, fosters self-talk and conversation, enables children to direct their own learning according to what interests them and allows them to participate at their own level (Crosse, 2007).
- Avoid the use of worksheets and vocabulary lists because they lack meaning and context.
- Prepare vocabulary lists for practitioners and support assistants in the children's first languages for each topic.

Teaching tip

Design your planning documents so that they include space for writing down what you want the children to learn (learning objective) and the language they will need to meet that objective (key vocabulary).

EAL and the EYFS profile

"We ensure that we always write down which language Sophia is using when we observe her."

At the end of the foundation stage a summative assessment must be completed for every child. In England this comes in the form of the EYFS profile, which provides an overview of the child's knowledge, skills and understanding across all seven areas of learning and development.

Teaching tip

Again, this highlights the need to enlist the help of bilingual support assistants to carry out observations and assist you with assessments so that you can form a clear idea of EAL learners' knowledge, skills and understanding across the curriculum.

Involving parents

The EYFS profile must be shared with parents. For those parents who speak little English it is helpful to set up a meeting with the help of a translator or bilingual support assistant so you can talk through the assessment with them.

Online resource: printable spreadsheet

The EYFS Profile Handbook highlights 'three aspects that are specific to the assessment' of EAL learners. These are:

- Development in their home language
- Development across areas of learning, assessed through their home language
- Development of English

It also states that attainment in the prime area of learning communication and language and the specific area of literacy 'must be assessed in relation to the child's competency in English'. All other areas of learning can be assessed in the child's home language (Standards and Testing Agency, 2014).

This has implications for the way you carry out observations and keep records. It highlights the importance of noting on observation sheets which language a child is speaking and responding to. Furthermore, it demonstrates the need to keep accurate records that will provide an overview of the child's progress in both their first language and English. One way of doing this is to create a spreadsheet for each area of learning with a list of development statements. Each time you observe a child demonstrating the knowledge, skills and understanding in a particular area note down the date and language next to the appropriate statement.

On good behaviour

"Whenever we gather the children for group time Abdul runs around and refuses to sit down."

Some EAL learners will find it difficult to settle in their new setting, and this may manifest in disruptive behaviour. Help these children by working to identify why they are behaving in such a way so that you can target additional support.

EAL learners have a lot to contend with, especially those who are completely new to a country and culture. It is therefore not surprising that some of these young children will struggle at first and react negatively to their situation. Help these children by:

- Observing them to see if you can identify any particular times of the day when their behaviour deteriorates. Can you spot triggers?
- Considering whether the activity you are asking them to do is too complex or difficult. Are you differentiating the task so that they can understand and contribute to the best of their ability?
- Creating a supportive learning environment where all children feel safe and secure and develop a positive self-image and self-esteem (see Idea 36).
- Setting up the learning environment so all children are able to independently access the resources and make the best use of their time.
- Taking a fair approach to behaviour management by having the same expectations for all children. Setting clear boundaries and taking a consistent approach will enable all children to learn about what is expected of them and avoid confusion.
- Creating pictorial rubrics that illustrate expected behaviour and pointing to these when asking children to follow instructions (see Idea 33).

Involving parents

Speak to parents about any behaviour issues you are experiencing within the setting, and ask if they have any problems at home. Take care not to vilify parents and make it clear that you are there to support them.

Identifying learning delay

"It's so difficult to tell if a child doesn't understand because I'm speaking in English, or if they don't understand because they just don't get it."

English as an additional language should not be categorised as a special educational need (SEN). However, it is possible that children learning EAL have SEN, and early years practitioners are met with the challenge of identifying the difference between a lack of understanding English and possible learning delay.

Involving parents

Soni (2013) recommends seeking parents' assistance when trying to identify potential learning delay by asking them to film their children speaking and listening at home so that practitioners can see their responses within a comfortable and familiar environment. This may help to distinguish between learning delay and lack of confidence. She also advocates inviting parents into the setting to play with their children while practitioners observe.

Every Child a Talker: Guidance for Early Language Lead Practitioners (DCSF, 2008) offers some very useful advice on how to identify learning delay in young EAL speakers. It highlights the following matters for concern:

- Children having difficulties understanding or using their first language.
- Children who have been in the setting for more than a term and have not yet begun to use or understand English.
- Children who have a history of hearing difficulties and middle ear infections.
- Children showing difficulty interacting non-verbally, for instance through pointing and making gestures.

All the time you are observing or working with a child who is new to English, consider whether they may be under stress or if the task is too difficult. Adapt the situation or task in order to reassess whether the child is struggling due to a learning need or the circumstances.

It is important to work together as a team when trying to identify a child with SEN, because a range of perspectives will enable you to form a more rounded picture of the child's development. This means ensuring that you communicate with parents, support staff and any outside professionals or agencies that may be involved.

Intervention

"Once we figured out that she had a special need we could put steps in place to help her."

Once you have identified that a child learning EAL has a special educational need (SEN) you will need to put steps in place as soon as possible to address this.

Different settings will have different procedures for supporting children with SEN, so you should speak to your SEN coordinator and refer to your setting's policy on SEN. Generally, in the first instance it is usual practice to put together an individual education plan that outlines the child's specific needs, what additional support they need, who will be providing the support and how often. In addition, it should set out a number of targets with a realistic review date to check on progress.

When planning intervention for a child learning EAL consider the following:

- If it is necessary to do focused language learning outside the classroom keep the sessions short and ensure that the task is related to the current topic or theme (Ofsted, 2013). Also try to take groups out rather than individuals to avoid children feeling targeted.
- Ensure that any additional activities for EAL learners are planned by the class teacher or lead professional in collaboration with support assistants (Ofsted, 2013).
- Enlist the help of a bilingual teaching assistant to support children who are failing to progress or are falling behind.
- Ask your local authority about opportunities for continuing professional development that specifically deals with helping EAL learners with SEN. Ensure that all support staff who work with these children have access to such training.

Involving parents

Be sensitive to differing cultural attitudes with regard to SEN. In some cultures people with disabilities and SEN are stigmatised and some parents may struggle to come to terms with their child having learning difficulties (British Council, 2015). Ensure that you put across the message that having SEN is nothing to be ashamed of, and work together with parents to devise some strategies that will help their child progress.

References

British Council (2015) *EAL Nexus: Learners with Special Educational Needs*. London, British Council. Accessed from: https://eal.britishcouncil.org/teachers/learners-special-educational-needs

Conteh, J (2012) *Teaching Bilingual and EAL Learners in Primary Schools*. London, SAGE

Crosse, K (2007) *Introducing English as an Additional Language to Young Children: A Practical Handbook*. London, SAGE

Department for Children, Schools and Families (DCSF) (2008) *Every Child a Talker: Guidance for Early Language Lead Practitioners*. Nottingham, DCSF Publications. Accessed from: http://webarchive.nationalarchives.gov.uk/20130401151715/https:/www.education.gov.uk/publications/eOrderingDownload/DCSF-00854–2008.pdf

Department for Children, Schools and Families (DCSF) (2009a) *Every Child a Talker: Guidance for Consultants and Early Language Lead Practitioners – Third Instalment*. Nottingham, DCSF Publications. Accessed from: http://www.foundationyears.org.uk/wp-content/uploads/2011/10/ecat_guidance_for_practitioners_31.pdf

Department for Children, Schools and Families (DCSF) (2009b) *Communication, Language and Literacy Development: Implications for Children for whom English is an Additional Language (EAL)*. Nottingham, DCSF Publications. Accessed from: https://www.lancsngfl.ac.uk/projects/ema/download/file/CLLD-EAL-Communication-Language-and-Literacy-Development-(CLLD).pdf

Department for Education (DfE) (2014) *Statutory Framework for the Early Years Foundation Stage*. London, HMSO

Frost, R *et al.* (2015) 'Word for Word'. *Nursery World*, 27 July: 21–23. London, MA Education

Hester, H (1990) *Patterns of Learning*. London, Centre for Literacy in Primary Education. Accessed from: www.clpe.org.uk

Huleatt, H (2013) *Block Play: Building Foundations for Literacy*. East Sussex, Community Playthings. Accessed from: www.communityplaythings.co.uk/learning-library/blog/2013/november/building-foundations-for-literacy

National Association for Language Development in the Curriculum (2011). *Developing Reading in EAL*. Accessed from: www.naldic.org.uk/eal-initial-teacher-education/resources/eal-literacy/

Office for Standards in Education (Ofsted) (2013) English as an Additional Language: A Briefing Paper for Section 5 Inspectors. London, HMSO. Accessed from: www.naldic.org.uk/eal-teaching-and-learning/outline-guidance/eal-ofsted

Palmer, S, and Bayley, R (2013) *Foundations of Literacy*. London, Featherstone

Siraj-Blatchford, I and Clarke, P (2000) *Supporting Diversity and Language in the Early Years*. Berkshire, Open University Press

Soni, A (2013) *EAL in the Early Years*. London, Featherstone

Standards and Testing Agency (2014) *Early Years Foundation Stage Profile: Handbook*. London, HMSO. Accessed from: www.gov.uk/government/publications/early-years-foundation-stage-profile-handbook

Further reading

Creative Activities and Ideas for Pupils with English as an Additional Language by Maggie Webster (London: Longman, 2011)

Distinguishing the Difference: SEN or EAL? by Susan Rosamond, Imtiaz Bhatti, Marion Sharif and Karen Wilson. (Sandwell: BASS, 2003) Available from: https://eal.britishcouncil.org/sites/default/files/document-files/Distinguishing%20the%20difference.pdf

English as an Additional Language in the Early Years: Linking Theory to Practice by Malini Mistry and Krishan Sood (London: Routledge, 2015)